Emerald

Eyes

Emerald

Eyes

By Lois Vogel-Sharp

Graphics, Design, and Editing
by Gary W. Sharp

Published by:

Lois Vogel-Sharp

2016

Visit us at our website:
KingofGloryOnline.org

Table of Contents

Preface

This book was written to show the amazing power of GOD and to make people aware that there are angelic beings in this world. We are in what is called the end times and not all angels are good. Mankind, whether he knows it or not, is part of the battle between good and evil that began in heaven when lucifer, the devil, decided he wanted to take over the throne of GOD ALMIGHTY! The battle continues to this very day and these demonic beings are looking to deceive as many people as possible. Until we recognize they exist we will continue to fall prey to their intention to destroy the image and likeness of GOD, Mankind. The method used to show this truth was by taking a real person who has experienced these beings. 1 Timothy 4:1 says but The Spirit speaks plainly that in the last time they shall depart one by one from the faith and they shall go after deceiving spirits and after the teachings of demons. The devil has a counterfeit for everything that GOD does and we need the gift discerning of spirits to know the difference. The word tells us in 1 John 4:1 do not believe every spirit but test them to see whether they are from God.

Introduction

Is it possible that we have the capability to actually speak with the spiritual world? I mean the angels of God and even the evil demonic beings. In the book of Enoch, he spoke to the beings from another realm as if it were normal! This emerald eyed beauty does the same thing and she attributes her ability as a God given gift called the discerning of spirits. This book is based on a true story. It is about a woman who followed the path of life as we all do but her destiny was not meant to be ordinary. She had no idea what was in store for her life as she lived each day expecting nothing unusual to happen. Our mind does not focus on a realm of reality that is as real as you and I are because we cannot see it with our natural eyes. I am talking about the spirit realm. The world that functions around us every day that we are not aware of unless we realize it actually exists. It not only exists; it plays an important part of our everyday lives. As you read this story and although the spirit realm that plays such an important role in this woman's life is partly conjecture, most of it is real. As crazy as it may seem this woman knows and sees how angels and demons are functioning around us all the time.

Before reading this story I have to say that in this year of 2016 there is much political correctness going on and people get offended over so many things these days. I have to tell you that I am not grammatically correct in this book because I refuse to capitalize the name satan. All words relating to God, Jesus or the Holy Spirit will be capitalized to show the due respect that I feel our God deserves. I cannot in good conscience capitalize the devil's name! In my opinion, he does not have the right to even have his name capitalized! Therefore, this book, will not be grammatically correct and I apologize to anyone who feels it should be. Enjoy this true story of Miss Emerald Eyes!

This is the first time this story has ever been told and it is all attributed to the Holy Spirit and the wonderful gifts He bestows upon the children of Almighty God, including this emerald-eyed beauty!

1

1. The Birth

It was a blistery cold day in January when heaven looked down upon the face of this green-eyed beauty who was born. She was chosen and set aside with a beauty mark that was placed on her cheek. Marcos who was the angel assigned to keep watch over this precious little girl had no idea that he would have his work cut out for him. Let me correct myself here, actually, he did, because God knows all things, therefore, the angels are told exactly what they have to deal with. The God of the universe had showered her with his blessings and she was meant to become someone very special. Her parents smiled as she gazed up with these piercing green eyes as if she could read your every thought. This black haired, green-eyed beauty was a bundle of joy and it pleased the God of the universe to put His breath of life into her soul. Marcos was so overwhelmed at his mission to keep her safe from harm's way. He was strong in character full of joy and had a lot of hope for her life. He looked at her and could see that God had special plans for her. He also knew that there was an adversary out there who hated all that God loved and he might have some battles to deal with in order to keep her protected. It was all right though because he had been trained very well and had been given much wisdom. His one concern was the lack of knowledge that so many human beings had when it came to spiritual warfare. He knew how hard it could be if the family involved was ignorant to the tactics of the enemy because then he could catch them unaware and knock them down. Marcos also knew that he could not go against the free will of man so he would pray diligently that this family would follow the ways of God and not the evil in the world. Even so, he was very thankful for his mission and appreciated the fact that this tiny little bundle of joy had great and marvelous things to do in her life.

In the hidden corners of darkness where evil existed hatred welled up as all the evil beings saw the beauty and grace that was bestowed upon this child. In secret, a plot was made to destroy the purpose of this child and to make sure she would find no joy in her life. Was there a reason behind this plot? None whatsoever except for the sheer satisfaction of tormenting one of

God's precious children. The evil beings were sure they would be able to get her, somehow, some way. It didn't care how long it might take but it was determined to stop whatever purpose she would have in accomplishing anything positive in her life. Had evil known that the hand of God's grace and mercy were on her it might have thought twice about devising any plans to destroy her. evil, although it could be clever, did not know everything and this was a hindrance in its existence. Her beauty was what really angered him and he figured if he could target in and use this beauty against her he would have a chance in turning her destiny around. After all, he was extremely skilled at influencing mankind into believing the world has all the answers to life's happiness and so began her life on a journey that she would have no idea of.

The sweet little child from the moment of birth was considered colic. She cried all the time as if something was tormenting her. This may seem a bit over the top but I assure you it is not and these things happen all the time in families where there is no real spiritual upbringing. This family had a grandmother who prayed all the time but there was no direct prayer going up to come against what this child was going through! There was one particular demon who came to actually torment her and his nasty task was to whisper negative words into her ear so her soul would hear it and receive it as truth. How can we hear such things from another realm? We are spiritual beings too, even though we have these human bodies, so our spirit picks many things up that are going on in that realm without us ever really knowing it. Anyway, back to this child. The nasty bulging eyed demon would go right up to her ear and say, "nobody loves you, everybody hates you." To describe how he looked you have to picture this in your mind. He would curl up the side of his mouth and then those bulging eyes would pop out even more as he sneered the words out. His face would contort into what we would call pure evil as it mischievously, not without excitement, shriveled its nose up and blurted over and over again, "nobody loves you, everybody hates you!" You may say how do you know this? Well, as the story goes she used to walk around the house when she was able to talk and actually say those words out loud. She would repeat them from time to time and where would she have heard them if not from some creepy, imp looking creature. Her parents never said it and to make that kind of a thing up is kind of far-fetched. This kind of thing goes on way more than we would like to believe. The only escape from it is to hear words of love and reassurance but most people do not realize that infants need to be spoken too in a positive way, not a negative way. This poor little green-eyed baby was from the moment of conception rejected as an unwanted pregnancy and this is where the enemy gets a foothold by our ignorance in not having a clue about the other side. If we realize anything from this story let us take a good look at this life and what the heck is really going on. What do we do about it? We seek the real truth about this world we live in and then trust our Father God to direct our path. If we do not believe that, we just deal with whatever comes our way in total defenselessness. Marcos, her guardian angel was upset about this because it was a spiritual uneasiness in the child that caused this and all he could do was sing songs of praise to try and comfort her. Her parents held her all the time trying to ease the discomfort she felt but there was not much that could be done. Her heart and soul had an uneasiness that nobody understood. evil laughed at her anguish and knew he had placed an insecure feeling within the spirit of the child because of an untimely pregnancy. Rejection was a big part of being human and evil threw it in people's faces as often as he could. Most times he would catch them unaware and keep them bound their entire lives because of circumstances that could not be helped or changed. Poor little miss green eyes so full of beauty and grace. Marcos felt for her but this was all part of being human and it was something he had to deal with as her guardian angel. His job was to intervene when evil would come in for the kill and it was not her time to die yet. He was on the alert because evil was targeting her already and Marcos could see this was going to get worse as time went on. evil was relentless and had no boundaries to follow because they left their home in total rebellion.

The parents named her Lilly Ann. Marcos looked into her green eyes and smiled because he knew how precious she was to God. It would be hard work for him but he was full of joy anyway. This was such a great purpose for him as for all the guardian angels to keep watch over the little ones. Each child of God has an angel assigned to them their entire lives but they never really

4

know because this spiritual realm has to be discerned with the eyes of the Spirit. Mom and Dad truly had their hand's full holding and cuddling her almost continuously. There seemed to be no comfort for this little soul without some human intervention. She was just a nervous child always wanting the assurance of love. The parents who loved her dearly sought advice from a physician who informed them that the child was healthy but just a nervous baby. There were no answers to her perpetual crying. Marcos knew very well what was happening in the world that he existed in. It was this spirit realm where all kinds of battles took place on a daily schedule. He had seen this over and over again, the insecurities of the human spirit, fear, doubt, and unbelief. The human killers as the angels of God called them. How well they knew this tactic of the evil one. All angels have confidence in the Almighty God and His healing power so he sang praises to God that night and she finally fell asleep in her mother's arms. She grew in the nurturing of her family with the love they gave her in spite of this flaw in her soul.

At a young age, evil showed its ugly face again. Here it was scurrying across the floor. The thing looked like a large bug with a human type face. It had wings sticking out its side so it had the ability to fly. It watched and waited for the moment to make its attack. Marcos stood by and watched as larian, the demons name, grinned. With an insatiable appetite to kill, his eyes opened wide and his mouth began to drool. It was quite disgusting to see but Marcos had to just stand by and wait. You might wonder why he did not just chase this creature away. Marcos could not because evil had certain rights in this world that man handed over to the devil in the Garden of Eden. The angels of God had to tolerate certain activities. The young child was playing and saw an object on the floor that was of interest and she put it in her mouth. As young as she was she had no idea of the danger. larian flew over quickly and shoved the object down her throat and she began to choke. evil watched, expecting death to occur because he had sent this spirit of death to suck the life out of the child. Marcos saw what this demon did and stepped into the picture. The only thing he was able to do was to try and influence her older sister to come and help. He whispered in her ear hoping she would spiritually receive the message. Thank God the child reached into her sister's throat and pulled out the object that was preventing the flow of air to the green-eyed beauty. Marcos was pleased and evil was frustrated. Marcos turned and looked at the demon of death who trembled and scurried away. How evil hated those eyes, those piercing green eyes that everyone raved about when they saw her. That was her attention getter. It was those eyes that everyone noticed no matter where she went and comments were made of how beautiful she was! evil was so jealous because at one time he was beautiful. All of his beauty left him because hatred had consumed his very being and there was nothing left but darkness and evil. His next target would be to destroy her eyes.

evil went into hiding and summoned his demon spirits. He ordered them to put a growth on her tiny little eye. Yes, that would be his plan to destroy those eyes by covering them with cysts so instead of seeing the beauty the focus would be on the growth. What a great plan he thought. The affliction was delivered and put on the child. It didn't show up for a few months because it was growing in secret. The irritation began and a small lump began to form. The child was so young she had no idea what was happening but mom knew it had to be taken care of. Marcos knew of the affliction but he was not able to prevent such things from happening. He knew as one of God's precious angels that this was all part of the purpose and plan to develop character in this child to have compassion and understanding for others. evil was in God's ultimate plan to mold this child into the faith believing Christian she was meant to become. Although God did not cause evil to happen he was quite aware when it did and was always ready to intervene somehow someway in order to fix the damage that evil would do. A doctor was needed in order to stop this cyst from growing and that is where the parents brought her. The green-eyed beauty needed an operation to remove this cyst. For a child who was this young to have to go into the hospital would be a very scary ordeal for her. evil was waiting and watching, gloating in his accomplishment to disrupt her life and afflict her beautiful green eyes. He was so thrilled that she would have to keep a patch over the eye for some time. He wouldn't have to look at those piercing eyes for a while and that accomplished its purpose as far as he was concerned. Marcos was with the child during the operation singing songs of praise as he usually did when things were very trying. Waking up from the anesthesia was the hardest part because she was very thirsty and wasn't allowed to drink any water for at least a few hours. She cried and cried and hated the patch that was meant to cover her God-given beauty. How innocent she was in all this and her entire life this memory never left her of the hospital stay and how humiliated she felt when they made her wear a diaper even though she was potty trained. She kept the vivid memory of the doctors coming in and placing the ether mask over her face. Marcos hated having to deal with the evil in this world but this was just the way it was and he knew that one day it would all be changed for the better. Until such time he was needed to help her get through life.

Life for this beauty was also filled with a lot of love. She had a grandmother who was filled with the love of God and did not feel embarrassed to profess her belief in Jesus. From a young child, Lilly heard all about Jesus and how much He loved her. Her grandmother had pictures of Christ all over the house and taught faith to the young girl. The grandmother would share stories of how God helped her. The children called her Grammy and she was blessed with musical talent. evil even tried to destroy the faith of the grandma by causing a car accident. Grammy had hit her head on the dashboard and two days later went deaf. In those days they didn't have the medical technology so the operation to possibly restore her hearing was very dangerous. As the story goes Grammy prayed to God and asked Him to restore hearing to her one ear. In return for this miracle, she would devote the rest of her life in daily prayer and thanksgiving. The prayer was answered and as a young child, she witnessed many times Grammy in prayer. Poor Grammy was tormented with crippling arthritis too but she never showed miss green-eyes her suffering. The only thing the little beauty saw was a woman of tremendous faith and that is what she learned and believed. Faith was a very powerful weapon against the enemy and emerald-eyes was given such a gift. How evil hated this child. He just had to find a way to destroy all this love and faith and the beauty he had to look at and envy. He really thought that he could take the beauty and turn it into a curse. That was the plan. Lust was a functioning sickness in the world and there was plenty of it around. It wouldn't be too hard to muster up some of it and focus it towards this beauty. Love and lust as far as the enemy was concerned was part of life and most people didn't know the difference. When you have natural beauty lust is always out there looking for you. It was only a matter of time before evil would have his way with her and emotionally abuse her for life. Plans were made in secret and the innocent child had no idea what was in store for her. Marcos knew that evil was plotting and he also knew that mankind had the ability to choose right and wrong every day and that was what this life was all about. He prayed that this child would make the right choices and not be tempted by the lusts of the flesh.

The child grew and loved to play outdoors. She loved to watch the tiny creatures as they scurried about doing their daily work. Her love of nature and the animals was wonderful. She would watch even the bugs and be amazed at the life they had. Her heart was full of desire to help any creature no matter how little or how big it was. She would find serenity and peace as she sat and wondered about life and creation. It may seem kind of strange but one day she noticed a tiny bumblebee floating in some water and her heart went out with a desire to save the poor drowning bee. Although she was afraid of the bee her desire to save it was greater and she got a stick and scooped it out. She watched the bee as it fought to live. She ran into the house and got a spoonful of honey hoping it would regain its strength. To her amazement, the bee stuck out what looked like a tongue and began to lick the honey. How thrilling it was for her to see this insect come back to life and eventually fly away. She was so happy to have saved its life. This was an instinct that was within her spirit to heal the hurting. It didn't matter to her whether it was an animal or a person she had the heart to save the hurting. The God of the universe had instilled this desire within her very soul and she just longed to reach out and touch the afflicted. Lilly had a very strong desire to pray for anything that needed help or deliverance. There were many times when Lilly would find a dead bird and literally lay her hands on it and pray for it to come back to life. I don't know about you but in my life, I do not think that is the norm for a child to even think of praying for something to come back to life and yet Lilly did this all the time. I guess one could say that the God of the universe gave her a knowing that death was not really the way things should have been and her soul

8

just thought of life rather than death. She would actually get frustrated when the bird did not get up and just fly away. I can't say for sure but I remember one day when Lilly found a sick bird that seemed to be ready to die and after she prayed she left the bird to go on to do other things. When she came back to check on the bird it was gone. If you ask me I think the bird got healed and flew away. She would sit and watch the ants for hours as they scurried about and one day she put a dot of paint on a few of the ants and waited to see if she saw them again. Sure enough the next day she saw the ants scurrying around and it brought a smile to her face to actually know that she was tracking down these tiny creatures. She was extremely interested in how life began and the miracle of it. All creatures to her were special and she just knew that God was the giver of all life and when it was taken away she felt that was wrong. Lilly had the God given wisdom to know that when God created something it was meant to live forever. She did not understand that in death there is still life because the spirit moves into the spiritual kingdom rather than this worldly kingdom. While Lilly enjoyed her times with nature she also saw many sad people who were struggling to deal with their lives. She just could sense when people were upset. It was so natural to her that she thought everyone could feel what others felt. The hurting were drawn to her like a magnet. Why? Because Lilly had the gift to touch the hurting.

evil saw this and decided to attack once again. He would use this love of life that she had and trick her. Everyone in the neighborhood knew how much she loved animals so one day the neighborhood boys called her and told her there was a baby kitten that was hurt in the garage next door. She went running as quickly as she could to help this kitten only to find a bunch of boys standing there waiting for her. As miss green eyes looked up at them, the older boy blurted out, "take off your clothes". This was the most devastating statement she had ever heard and she became panicked. Marcos was right by her side as he glared at the spirit of lust who was standing next to the boy whispering in his ear. One thing about this green-eyed beauty, she may have been shy but when confronted she would stand her ground if need be. The humiliation was almost impossible to take but her spirit was strong and she would never just listen to a command like that.

9

Tears welled up in her eyes as she began to cry in despair. The boys got frightened and ran home. Nobody can actually say what startled them, but I believe the glare from Marcos spooked the demon and the boys. Little Lilly ran home as quickly as she could and told her mother. Her mom's advice was to stay away from them and don't fall for any of their lies.

evil was not happy at this failure so he connived another plan to upset her life. This time, he would take her desire to heal the hurting and make her believe she was the cause of their pain. Her puppy caught distemper and became very ill. In the middle of the night, she woke up and wanted to go to the puppy to help. She felt terrible watching the poor puppy suffer this way. There was nothing she could do. While she was there death entered and the puppy died right in front of her. She had never seen death before and it was very upsetting to her. She actually watched the life of the puppy leave, as the body of the puppy went limp. This was very emotional for her at this young age and she cried her heart out. She thought, "why did death have to be?" Why couldn't she just pray and see them come back to life? Death was not something she could accept. She saw only life around her and death was so hurtful that she had a hard time believing in it. evil watched and was exceedingly proud when he made her believe it was because of her the animal died. What happened that made her feel this way? This creepy, imp looking being, flew over to Lilly and spoke right into her ear. With a repetitious chanting, he kept saying over and over again "Look what you have done, you made your puppy die. Look what you have done you made your poor little puppy die." Lilly felt those words right down in her soul and took them to heart! Marcos hung his head because he knew that death was a part of life but it was not the plan of God from the beginning. The disobedience of man brought death into the world and it was not very pleasurable to have to watch this. What Lilly did not know was that God was ultimately in control over death and life and Lilly had an anointing given to her from God and as the story continues we will see just what I am talking about!

The family also had a canary and it just so happened that the day the bird died this beauty was there once again to see it. As a matter of fact, the bird was sick and there she was wanting to

10

help again. She placed her tiny hands into the cage to pick up the sickly bird and she looked down at it and was saddened. How she wished she could just pray and make it all right. The next moment the bird went limp and the life was gone. How terrible for her to see this again and have been near the bird. The thought immediately went through her mind that she caused this. evil whispered in her ear that she had the touch of death. Marcos was so angry but he had to stay back and allow this to happen. Her sisters began to make a joke out of it too. They would tell her that she had the touch of death. evil was trying to convince her of this to instill fear so she would not pray for healing. Her heart just felt the need to believe for life and not accept death. She would find dead birds in the yard and ask God to heal them and bring them back to life but her prayers always went unanswered. She found it very hard to accept a God of love being able to sit back and watch His creation die. No! she would not accept death even though it was a reality. Her little spirit just could not believe it. Life was too precious to her and she would always believe for healing no matter what the outcome would be. That was the kind of God she loved. He was a life giver, not a life taker. Her faith was amazing. From a very early age, she began to see the workings of evil and sensed without any real knowledge that there was an enemy out there trying to upset her. Whenever she would do something kind for someone it always seemed she got hurt. evil would make sure she tripped or scraped herself somehow. Lilly knew in her very being that evil was watching and wanting to create harm.

I remember one day when she was playing outside. She was walking with a glass of juice in her hand and all of a sudden, if you would have been able to see in that spirit realm, it was a dark creepy looking thing that ran in front of her. At that exact moment, she lost her footing and fell to the ground. Marcos broke the fall but this ugly evil thing was so fast and I have to say this because the guardian angels do not stop every attack that happens to us. evil is here and evil does attack and we all go through things in this world that we wish had never happened. Lilly tumbled to the ground and the glass shattered all over the place. One would have thought she should have gotten cut from the broken glass but she only got a scraped knee thanks to Marcos.

Green-eyes looked around as if she sensed something in the spirit realm that was there. Marcos was pleased to see her spiritual senses coming to life as she matured. She knew of the evil presence that lurked about and it depressed her. She had no real spiritual knowledge and did not know what to do about the evil but she sensed its presence. She was extremely shy and oppressed with this insecurity in her life. All of her talents were hidden under her beauty because she was too quiet to express any of them. When people would look at her beauty and no matter where she went they looked, she would withdraw into herself. Instead of accepting the praise that was given her she would reject it. She feared what people thought because she wanted to be loved by all. She was learning in her life and it would be some time before she would overcome these insecurities that plagued her. She continued to see love from her family and her grandmother kept telling her how special she was. She would tell her that she was given talents from God and the child held all these truths in her heart. She knew within herself that she had been chosen for something but her shyness just hindered her every step of the way. The God of the universe had called her and no evil would be able to prevent her purpose unless she chose to follow it. evil did not give up. It knew about human nature and it was counting on the flesh to mess things up for her. The teachers in her school loved her and constantly pointed her out as a beauty. They would praise her for her academic abilities and always would make mention of those beautiful eyes. This attention made her feel uncomfortable because she wanted to sit in the back of the room and not be noticed. It just didn't happen that way because the more she wanted to hide the more attention she got. The children in the class picked her to be the class president and even the children in her class who were the known troublemakers loved her. They would sit down next to her and tell her all about their troubles. She was a natural at showing compassion and helping them to feel better about themselves. Lilly did not realize that this ability was a God given a gift and the Spirit of God was already using her to reach out to the hurting souls. The special feeling, she had each time a person would walk away feeling better about themselves made her enjoy helping them. Her desire to be loved by all created an uncomfortable feeling

12

within her because she always felt the need to be perfect. How she would cry when she would receive a 99% on a test instead of a 100%. I guess you could say she was a perfectionist. Her beauty, her smarts, and her popularity kept her feeling this need to maintain this position of perfection in the eyes of everyone. Lilly was so insecure in her own soul that she did not really believe she was accepted unless she was the perfect person. Lilly was above average in everything she did but her reading skills could use improvement. She never enjoyed reading even though her mother and sisters all loved to read. For Lilly to read a book it had to be really interesting to her because it just would not hold her attention. It was expected of her to be tops in her class in everything she did. As the leader of the reading group, she felt very pressured to excel in this area of speed reading. The others in the group could read quicker than she could and this was embarrassing for her. Lilly had access to the answers as the leader of the reading group. Many times in this life we have no idea of what is happening in the spiritual realm but let me show you what happened. There are many unseen beings that go about looking for a soul to steal you might say. Spirits speak to us whenever they see the opportunity as we have human frailties. This one particular demonic being saw his opportunity when the pressure to perform hit Lilly. He came right up to her face and boldly spoke to her. With an arrogance and an attitude of anger and rebellion he point-blank told her, "if you do not ace this test you will look like the biggest fool in this classroom because they will all know how stupid you really are." The pressure she felt to perform on this high level allowed this cheating mode to begin. This was the evil one intervening but human nature chooses between right and wrong and little miss green eyes began to cheat out of desperation to maintain the high standards that were expected of her. She was not as skilled as the others in the group so instead of being honest she cheated on the tests. Guilt hit her soul as she knew she was not as skilled as the marks were showing her to be. At night she would think that God was going to strike her down with lightning because of her dishonesty. She would apologize to God every night but be angry at herself for being a cheat. The sad part about this is she was a very smart child and didn't need to cheat. Maybe she would not have gotten the highest marks but she certainly would have done well. This is how the human spirit is. The insecurities that the evil knows so well about us can cause us to make decisions that are not always honest. Why does life have to put these perfection pressures on us so we feel the need to have to be dishonest in order to live up to the standards we think we should? Anyway, Lilly had to deal with this. She was in a battle between doing the right thing or taking the easy way out and cheat to look better. Marcos grieved a bit knowing this was all so unnecessary. He knew it was part of her growing up and learning to accept herself for who she really was not for who people wanted her to be. I have to say here that Lilly did finally make the choice to do the right thing and admitted to the others in the group that she was having a bit of a hard time keeping up. She just slowed the pace down and took the time to read and learn. She felt good pushing aside her discomfort and choosing to just accept herself for her abilities, not her trying to perform for all to see. Her conscience had won because in her soul she knew right and wrong and wanted to please God rather than herself. Lilly was not a cheat and had a very high-grade average without ever cheating. This time, demonic influence coupled with the need to be accepted made Lilly cave into temptation. She never forgot how humiliated and guilty she felt in choosing to do what she did. If you take a minute here to evaluate this spiritual kingdom you can look back and actually find out what brought about all this angelic activity and demonic activity.

We are now entering the gates of heaven and will watch the unfolding of the battle that took place before we were ever created. In the beginning, God and that is disputed by scholars who say that we came into existence by a big bang theory. Anyway, on the throne, His throne may I say, was God Almighty! Picture looking around at the beauty of this place where precious stones were everywhere adorning the throne and majesty of heaven! The glitter of gold on the streets as the radiance shined from every precious stone imaginable. The glimmer of all the shining gems not to speak of the light beaming from God Himself. The Trinity all sharing one mind and one accord as they spoke about the chatter going on all around heaven. lucifer the most beautiful angel ever created shined his beauty which God had given him. The power and abilities went beyond anything we could imagine.

Perfection in all it's glory. Heaven, yes it's heaven. Rumblings from the clouds in the distance made everyone aware that something was going on and everyone was on alert! Marcos gives account on what began to happen in heaven throughout eternity. This place known to the angels as their dwelling place was under siege. The once Holy place and perfect place without spot, wrinkle or blemish was now looking to be taken over. Who would have the audacity to challenge the Most High God. Whisperings were going on throughout the Kingdom and from my recollection angels were being asked to join forces with who? lucifer? "lucifer," did you say, yes, "lucifer." God's right-hand angel is trying to wage a war in heaven? This cannot be true! Who would be so prideful that they would actually think they could take God down? It was lucifer and he went about recruiting one-third to his side. Unbelievable! Get a good picture of this darkness trying to consume the brightness of heaven. Dark clouds swelling up, encircling the outer perimeters of heaven, engulfing the angels who have rebelled and are about to attack. Since angels cannot die the battle involves power and who has the greatest power of all. Picture angels flying everywhere as they attack one another with such force that the heavens themselves shook. lucifer had business on earth and this battle actually overturned much of the earth which had to be replenished when Adam was created. The powers that be were all fighting to maintain control of heaven and hurl out every evil angelic being that turned against God. The warrior angels were fiercely stripping the unfaithful angels of their power and hurling them with such force beyond the gates of heaven. Michael took lucifer who is now satan and threw him like lightning. They lost all they had and it was one of the biggest mistakes made in the history of the universe and eternity. Never to be part of God's Kingdom ever again. No wonder why they have such anger. They truly blew it and their vengeance is on mankind who was created in the image and likeness of God. That really ticks them off. Now you can see why the devil has it in for us and actually he is now in the process of taking over the earth. He will get so far and again he will be beaten down. Now that we have a picture of what happened back then, we can continue in the life of this chosen child who has the ability to see these beings and to do miracles for God right here on earth!

15

It was so hard for Lilly to stand up for herself when confronted by others who were cruel. She found it very hard to accept the fact that there were people who were not nice. There was a boy in her class who I believe really liked her but had a strange way of showing it. He would sit next to her and every day he would punch her in her arm. He would get this smirk on his face and Lilly could see there was something not right about this. What could possibly be the reason he would just punch her arm? It would really hurt and because she didn't want to hurt his feelings she just sat there and let him hit her. On her way home from school she would go over it in her head and get mad at herself for not saying anything. It was so frustrating because at home with the neighborhood kids she had a bit of a temper and if she got mad everyone would go home because they knew not to get her angry. In school, it was quite the different story. She was shy and very easy going but at home, she was able to be herself and express her true feelings. She had this secret side of her that nobody really knew except her family and close friends. This made it all the more difficult for her to let down her guard and allow people to see the real Lilly. She was a sweet spirited child but did have her moments of anger and frustration like we all do. I would have to say she took people and situations very personally and this sensitivity was what she was all about. Her open heart caused her pain and it also allowed her to feel for others. The problem with Lilly was she would allow people to push her around until she finally would blow up. The boy who kept punching her arm walked home with her one day and again punched her arm and this was just one of those days when Lilly had enough. She became so upset that she did not care what he would think of her and in anger and frustration yelled, "you better never punch my arm again." Lilly was shaking from the adrenaline rush she felt and felt bad for him but she just blurted out those words in anger. He never did it again! Marcos knew she had to get a grip on these feelings and learn to let them go instead of taking them to heart. To feel for others was a gift but to hold the hurts inside would only cause sadness and that was not a good thing to hold onto. Holding back your emotions rather than expressing them only binds us up. Human nature, Marcos knew it could be a blessing and a curse at the same time. This was the area that evil

16

was able to target in on because it was so vulnerable and lacked so much knowledge that he pretty much had free reign on most human beings. Green-eyes was no exception to being part of the human race and all the issues that go along with it. He just watched her day and night gloating at her guilt and her inability to express her true self. A child of many talents but closed within herself. It was all just buried within her heart and soul wanting to burst out but unable to because of her fear of rejection. So she went through much of her elementary school years living this double life striving for perfection.

Her beauty had all the boys interested in her. She loved the attention but didn't really believe anybody loved her for who she really was. Then evil came up with a plan to stifle the green-eyed beauty. One day Lilly was not able to read the blackboard anymore without it being blurry. She had to squint in order to see the letters and the next thing you know she needed glasses. What a blow to her beauty. evil laughed because now her eyes would be covered. The little beauty hated the glasses and was very embarrassed about them. She only put them on to read the board and then would hide them in the desk. This just made her feel more insecure about herself and her trying to be perfect in the eyes of everyone else. There was nothing she could do about it because without the glasses she could not read the board. This was all part of the afflictions of the flesh in this imperfect world we live in. She was very skilled in math and maintained almost a perfect 100. By the time she was in 6th grade her anger at herself for the few times she had cheated caught up to her and she could no longer accept anyone's praise of her. They voted her class president once again as it was every year and she refused to take the position. She just felt she wasn't worthy of it. evil once again stepped into the picture picking up on her human frailty. He sent a spirit of insecurity to hang around her. Marcos was angry because now he had to watch this demon push himself on her and try to convince her of these feelings that she was already experiencing. He knew that it was up to Lilly to stop this and he had no right to intervene. He prayed all the time for her to see what was going on. His faith told him that one day she would find victory. In spite of all this insecurity and now these feelings of depression Lilly graduated sixth grade with a 96 average and that was with no cheating. I want to say here that it wasn't that she cheated all the time. She was very smart but on a few occasions with the reading she had to cheat in order to do as well as it was expected of her. This was all part of growing up and making choices. The emerald-eyed beauty still had no idea what her life was meant to be as she struggled to find her identity.

Time away from school was where she really opened up her eyes to begin sensing this realm in the spirit that we cannot see with our natural eyes. There was no doubt that when she would show kindness towards others some kind of an affliction would befall her. It was so obvious to her that this made her begin to know of this other world. She knew that it was not a coincidence when these situations would happen. Fear would try to come upon her and she would think something bad was going to happen. Even though she felt unloved in her life she knew there was good and evil. How she would hate that there was some unknown force out there just looking to hurt people. One day after she had been kind to one of the girls who lived down the block and gave her some money to go buy some candy she was walking down the street and a branch sprung out and hit her right near her eye. If it had been another half an inch she would have been hit right in the eye. Marcos was there to help prevent this from happening because he watched the evil spirit jump onto the tree and grab the branch. Marcos was waiting and watching to see what the demons plan was and then in a moment of time, he flung the limb out towards her beautiful green eyes in an attack to damage them. The branch came flying very quickly and Marcos just in time reached out to grab it. It hit near the eye but did not reach the eye and Lilly was protected from what could have been a real blow to her eyes. It did hit her and it left a mark but it did not do the damage the demon really intended for it. Little green-eyes had no idea that her guardian angel had prevented an affliction. Marcos was a good protector but those demons can sure be quick he thought. This was not the end of the evil attacks.

Although these attacks were what we call everyday normal living they were from a realm of the spirit that most people are unaware of. Unless you have your spiritual eyes open most of these attacks will go unnoticed and will be accepted as part of life. Is there any way of actually stopping these demonic beings? They can be thwarted but only if you know they exist. Why would you pray or stand against something if they were unknown? These forces of darkness are unseen but not unreal. This spiritual realm continues every day to manipulate and attack and destroy the image of God daily. They have no other purpose but to latch on to people to do their agenda. Their agenda is anything from conducting their perverted personalities to inflicting pain and emotional suffering. Do you get it that they have no other means to deploy their plans accept by using human being bodies? They are floating around planet earth without bodies. Without a body, they are just a spirit. With a body, they can move to accomplish their goal of destroying God and His creation. Nobody is free from their attacks. The only way of escape is to see them for who they are and deal with them. Jesus dealt with them and they would leave as He commanded them to do. Lilly still had no real idea of what to do with them or even if they really existed. It was something she felt within her soul but had no real knowledge about.

Her soul began to be tormented at night with nightmares. There was one specific demonic spirit that was sent to harass her while she slept. Marcos saw it every night and stood by her side praising God while this little creepy thing would sit by her ear and whisper all sorts of scary thoughts into her spirit. The demon would tell her that nobody really loved her and she was all alone without anybody accepting her for who she was. These lies would spark nightmares of rejection that would wake the child up in a cold sweat screaming for her mother. She would sit up with her eyes wide open and still be asleep in this nightmare. Mom would come in to comfort her and after what seemed to be forever she would finally wake up. She hated to go back to sleep for fear of another nightmare. Only time and maturing made the dreams stop. The dreams were so upsetting that Lilly still remembers them to this day. One had to do with a train chasing her around and then this scary lady would walk up to her face and ask her what was the matter. The lady was so creepy and scary that Lilly would go into panic mode. It sounds silly now but back when Lilly was still young it was very scary for her. She would lay in bed and feel like the walls were closing in on her too. Lilly would just lay in bed and feel fear as she looked around her room. She sensed evil and did not know what to do about it. This was the problem with most people. Fear and evil were around and nobody knew what to do about it. The creepy impy creatures were roaming about all the time waiting to instill fear on mankind. The only weapon is perfect love which the bible tells us casts out fear. Unless we know that we are loved by God we will live in fear. The Truth is vital in this world of deception and lies. When someone has the gift to see these spiritual beings most people think they are crazy. Why? The unknown scares us and we cannot accept it so we create our own self-defense against it which is to believe this world does not exist.

Visits to Grammy helped her grow in faith and trust. Grammy would sit for hours and tell stories of a God who answered prayers and who loved them. Although Lilly did not understand she listened and learned and these seeds were planted in her little heart. She received this truth because it made sense that if there was evil there had to be good. Since good and evil were the opposite they both would play an important part of life showing us that the path to peace would always be on the trail of seeking the goodness of God.

2. What You Can't See

In the lower chambers of darkness, the prince of darkness sat and contemplated how he would continue to torment this child of beauty. He summoned all of his lustful demons and they sat and discussed how they would go about the earth seeking whom they may devour. One perverted spirit glared at the prince and said that he had been watching this emerald-eyed beauty and would like to take a stab at trying to seduce her and pull her into the world of lust and perversion. The prince focused on this spirit with his fiery red eyes and with a stern voice told the spirit, "no." Another more demonic looking demon stepped up to the prince and said, "I know I can use her beauty against her and her desire to be loved and definitely bring her into the world of torment." The prince once again stared into the face of this demon and said, "no." The chamber was filled with thousands of lustful and perverse demons. The plan was to indiscreetly target her and catch her unaware. He gazed around the chambers for the perfect demon to fulfill this task. With his piercing red eyes, he searched for one quiet, but determined spirit who would have a lustful desire to follow her for years until she would fall flat on her face. It didn't matter how or when but the goal was to discredit her and turn her away from the Lord. Beauty was a gift from God but how well the evil one knew that such a gift could easily be used for his purpose rather than to shine the light of the Lord. The prince trembled at the thought of the Lord. He shuttered knowing in his soul that his fate was already sealed. Anger welled up inside of him as he pictured the compassionate green eyes of this child. Then he noticed falon who was standing in the far corner of the chamber with all of his charm and charisma. They both stared into each other's eyes and it was settled. falon was the chosen demon to accomplish this task for the prince of darkness. Everyone congratulated him for being chosen. The prince nodded and falon was off to roam the earth.

A special messenger from God was sent to Marcos to update him on this meeting of the demons that had just taken place. How disgusting Marcos thought. He had a hard time understanding why any of God's angels would have chosen to

21

follow after darkness rather than light. It didn't make sense to him how the demons could find pleasure in tormenting the likeness and image of God, human beings. What a sad fate for them all he thought. He also knew there was no redemption for them and their fate was sealed for eternity. falon who was chosen to destroy little Lilly was trained in the same group of angels, as was Marcos. Marcos knew he was quite capable of doing some major damage and he would have to be on his guard continuously in order to protect Lilly from harm. Marcos wasn't afraid that let's just say he was concerned about the human desire of the flesh to feel loved. He knew that green-eyes was insecure and how easy it is to mistake lust for love when you are young and naive. falon didn't waste any time in his plot to bring her into perversion. Although he had been given no specific time to accomplish this task he was determined to get the job done. falon did his best to entice her into every form of sexual perversion there is, to no avail. Without going into detail with the biblical perversions, on one occasion, when falon recruited a few more demons to help him in his quest to bring down Lilly, Marcos made sure she would not fall into any traps set by him and made it loud and clear in an almost audible voice that Lilly could actually hear when he yelled out "do not do that"! With the moral upbringing of Lilly and her sensitivity to the spirit world this precious beauty actually heard the voice of Marcos that day as he stepped in to help her stay out of any temptation from the evil one. She was awed by the voice that she knew was spoken from the other side and she knew from the authoritativeness of the voice that she should not do what was forbidden. Let's just say falon's attempt to really pervert this child failed. Her moral upbringing and the voice of her guardian angel prevented what could have been her downfall for sure. She knew for sure from that moment that there was a spirit realm that was operating around her. falon's attempt to bring her into perversion never again happened but in his anger at his failure he tried to give her nightmares about the incident. Wow! The lengths evil will go to destroy the children of God. falon knew she was too pure for him to succeed at anything so perverted so he would have to stick to the regular human lust to keep her from becoming a woman of God. Marcos and falon caught each other's eye during this episode and when falon glared at Marcos his spirit trembled as he felt the presence of the Almighty God. Marcos just looked with all the light of heaven behind him and was saddened to remember the time before the fall of the angels from grace.

Let's go up to heaven for a moment and see the angelic in action. During these episodes of trial and error, there resounds in heaven all manner of prayer and intercession for the souls down here on earth. With so much evil to deal with on earth, it is nice to take a few moments and picture heaven. Angels gathered together with the sparkling of the all the jewels that are everywhere. The total feeling of peace and the knowing that all is well in spite of how trying it may be down here. A place of such beauty we can hardly imagine it. The flowers and the trees are all perfect. There are no tears and no hate either. No imperfections at all and total freedom in who you are. Makes me want to go right now. With rejoicing and singing the angels watch and know that the God of the universe has a plan and a purpose for each child born. A specific angel is assigned to each child and unless the child as an adult rejects God and turns to the evil that angel is with them their entire life. The sole purpose of the angel is to protect in time of trouble but to never go against the freedom of man to choose his own destiny. The most frustrating part for the angels is when people make wrong choices and suffer the consequences because of it. They are full of joy for the most part but they do have feelings very similar to us. They just know how to control their feelings and never allow them to take over the peace they have while standing in the very presence of God. Marcos at this point was angry. He knew falon personally and was emotionally upset by his attempt to destroy this innocent child of God. His question was why we couldn't all just love one another?

Lilly continued to grow and learn about life. She spent a lot of time outdoors observing the animals and just loving nature. You could definitely say she was learning to realize more about life as she matured each day. Lily did have her moments of joy too as she grew but there was most definitely evil lurking about trying to find a way to get her. I remember the day when Lilly was outside playing with the neighborhood boys and one of them had a pocket knife. They were throwing the knife at the tree and watching it stick into the bark. Lilly was fascinated by this and asked if she could try and throw it. Marcos looked around at that moment to check and see if there was anything lurking about and he saw nothing so he felt relieved. Lilly picked up the knife and threw it at the tree and in that moment of time there came from behind the branch what I would say looked like a gremlin. It had a smirk on its face as it grabbed the knife and flung it back at Lilly. Marcos with all the speed the Lord had given him pushed the flying knife and it hit Lilly just above her right eye. It hit and fell to the ground making a small flesh wound. Lilly began to cry more out of fear rather than pain because the knife did not penetrate it actually bounced off. It was another attack on Lilly's eyes to try and deform them. I'll tell you if it wasn't for Marcos and his skills Lilly would be in a lot of trouble. The favor of God was on her but she still had no idea of this. Her desire to help others was growing as she experienced more and more of life. These incidences that continued to happen made her faith grow as she would see that someone was protecting her from any real harm.

Grammy was a real prayer warrior who was intervening on behalf of all the grandchildren every day. I do believe that if it were not for those continuous prayers the evil would have been able to get the best of her and even with all the prayers and supplication before the Lord, Lilly developed allergies. Nobody knew it at the time but she started to get dark circles under her beautiful green eyes. She would feel fatigued at times and depressed but not understand why. There were many days when she just could not bring herself to go to school and deal with the day. She would stay home and sit in bed all day and think about life and the sorrows of it. How desperately she wanted to feel loved but didn't. She was always looking to perform and remain that perfect person that everyone thought she was. This was just too much stress on her and these allergy symptoms were the result of it. There seemed to be no relief from the attacks on the eyes or some sort of a lustful situation that would bring itself into the picture.

falon waited for just the right moments to make his perverse moves on her expecting her to give into temptations of the flesh or give in because of embarrassment. Let me tell you about the man of the cloth who was a friend of her Godparents. He was always hanging around the children and this one particular

24

day Lilly was sitting next to him and she was feeling rather uncomfortable. falon didn't even have to do anything because this man already had a lustful problem with children. He looked at Lilly and smiled and asked her to come sit on his lap. She just knew in her heart that something was not quite right about his affection. She could see right into his soul because when he smiled it was not a normal smile that one would give. This smile had a meaning behind it. The meaning that was very obvious to Lilly was "come here little girl, I have this interest in you that should not be. The average child would have no idea but Lilly just knew something was wrong with him. She could not see at that point in her life the animal-like creature that was sitting right on his shoulder smiling right along with this supposed man of God. She got up and left the room making sure to stay away from him. falon was enraged at her keen sense and became more determined to crush her like a bug. How he hated the innocence she projected. Marcos was so pleased with her intuition in picking up on this spiritual realm. Lilly still did not realize the beauty she possessed and how it brought the worst out in men who could be influenced by the evil one. She couldn't escape because the boys lusted after her in school too. There was one particular boy in her art class who was very much influenced by sexual curiosity and he relentlessly tormented her every day. I have to say that falon played a major role in this because the boy just sat there and was moved by the demons every influence. falon loved it. He got someone who he could control and really make her sweat with anxiety. The boy sat across from her and began to ask her all kinds of sexual questions. He asked her one day if she was still a virgin. Lilly wanted to die on the spot. She didn't even know how to answer him; she was so humiliated. He then proceeded to tell her he would love to have sex with her. He would bend over and look up her dress and then tell her what color underwear she was wearing. It was almost more than she could handle. Lilly knew this was not normal behavior but had no idea it was an actual demon manipulating this young man. It was so out there that Lilly was so upset she had no words to even say. The demonic pressure that was being thrown at her was unbelievable to her very soul. She could not make any sense of how this boy could even speak to her this way. One thing she did know and that was it was

25

downright evil. It stressed her out so much she lived in fear of having to go to this class and deal with this. How she hated to go to the class every day and have to deal with this humiliation on a daily basis. She just did not have the nerve to tell on him or tell him to shut up. Her insecurity kept her from saying anything. To top off the humiliation she was feeling the teacher picked her one day to sit in front of the class and have everyone draw her. She had to pose with her legs stretched out front so they could draw the curves. She was dying on the inside and of course, this boy just kept smiling as he lusted after her body. falon was in hysterics at this sight and was proud of his accomplishment to sexually harass her. Lilly would go home and cry and tell no one of her agony. Marcos felt for her but could not stop the harassment. It was up to Lilly to stop this but she didn't. The boy continued to humiliate her by telling her that her breasts were too small. The demon was just doing anything to bring her down and the words were not even truth. Lilly took that to heart and decided she was going to exercise them to make them grow larger. Poor Lilly she was still young and her breasts were not developed yet. Peer pressure can be a real hard thing to deal with for a teenager. Words can destroy when a person is not strong enough in their own person. She was convinced that she wasn't going to be normal so she felt the need to improve her body and all because of one selfish insensitive young man who was full of lust. This attack touched the heart of God and His mercy came on the scene when for some odd reason the boy got transferred into another class. When Lilly came into class and saw that he was gone and that he had been transferred she was stunned and was grateful. Lilly did not feel like it was a coincidence that he left. She could sense that there had been an intervention on her behalf. Lilly was relieved and that pressure ceased for the time being.

We all desire to be beautiful but did you ever realize the problems you can have when you have been given a beautiful face? Who would think that there could be so many problems? Lilly was learning very quickly that most people were not for real but were out for their own self-interests not caring if they stepped on someone to get there. In her innocence, Lilly continued to be forgiving of those who humiliated her and looked to hurt her. She was growing up being taught by her parents to show love and kindness to others and because of this she always looked to find the best in people even when they were being inconsiderate. She had neighbors who lived down the block from her who had two girls who were the same age as her and her sister. They would come and play with her but their family life was anything but normal. One particular day she went down to their house to play with them and as she approached the house they came to the window and told her they had been beaten by their stepfather. They showed her the welt marks on their legs from the belt that was used to hit them with. Lilly was shocked to see this and learned that day of the harsh cruelty man can bestow on others. She felt empathy for them but knew in her heart there was nothing she could do to help them. Her heart broke and she felt anger at the cruelty of this man. Deep within her soul, a desire welled up to want to make right the injustices of life. Compassion was becoming part of her spirit as she would see the neighborhood children living their lives in a way that she knew was just not right. She could sense the evil that was very much a part of people's everyday lives.

A situation happened in her neighborhood that really creeped her out at a young age and left an everlasting impression on her. Marcos knew these were all of life's learning lessons and how he hated the world and the way it was. Remember Marcos is a part of that spiritual realm that we as human beings are not always aware of so he sees first-hand what is actually happening when demonic activity is causing a situation to happen. Lilly heard that her neighbor across the street committed suicide by breathing in the fumes from the car. Not too long after this the neighbor who lived two houses down from her hung himself in the attic one day. This really made her think because it seemed a bit too coincidental to have two people living so close who both killed themselves. Marcos knew it was the demon of suicide who goes about looking for a distraught soul who will listen and take their life. Lilly was very much moved with fear as she thought about how someone could take his or her own life like this. It just seemed scary to her to think about death this way. How she hated death and the whole thought of the body dying. It just didn't seem right to her for life to have to end when God created it to live. Lilly knew that the spirit would go and be with God when someone died but with suicide nobody really seemed to know if they would make it into heaven. This bothered her and gave her an uneasy feeling. We all are told that God loves us if we have families that teach us that but Lilly just couldn't seem to get a grip on that. The message of a loving God just was not sinking into her heart the way it should have. The insecurity that was such a part of her convinced her that nobody loved her. How could they, for she was not the perfect little child, that people thought she was? The problem was that Lilly didn't love herself. She did not know what real love was all about. Watching people and their phony ways did not help her in realizing that God was different. What Lilly didn't realize was that the love she had for others and the desire to help was from God and that was what He was all about. She was just too young yet to see this truth and so she continued to develop in character as a caring sincere person. Lilly knew that most people lacked in love including herself and yet she wanted to bring love to everyone. Life was very precious to her and she would spend a lot of time just thinking what it was all about. She expected nothing but the best because within her heart and soul she had the knowledge of her Father God and His goodness. Lilly was so blessed. Marcos would get so excited with anticipation knowing the day would come when she would mature and realize who she was as a child of the Most High God. You see the angels know that as God's children we are perfected into the image of Jesus and that takes time so they stand by us through it all. Through the sufferings and the sorrows, they stand with us knowing the day will come when we will achieve the goal that God desires for us. Some of us will fall on our faces many times. Some may get shot in the battles of life but as a child of God even if we lose our life down here we still win because our spirit goes to be with our Father God. The more knowledge we have the easier it is to stand up against the evil that lurks about seeking whom it may devour. Lilly still had no idea how hard evil was trying to knock her out of her purpose for her life.

falon hated her, he couldn't wait for his purpose in destroying her to be accomplished. Lilly who hated death so much and wanted to prevent it from happening had a life threatening experience one day that gave her a taste of it and one that she never forgot. The family had gone to the beach, the ocean to be exact. She and her two sisters were playing in the waves having a great time. They were jumping up and down, as each wave would hit them. It was a bit scary for Lilly because the force of the waves could be rather strong and you really had to get a grip on your feet so as not to get knocked over. Lilly looked up and could see a large wave approaching her and fear hit her as the wave knocked her off of her feet. She was being dragged by the fury of the undercurrent and she could not get her bearings so she could find her way up. Confusion hit her mind as she opened her eyes to see. She didn't know which way was up or down and her mind told her she might drown. What seemed like an eternity really only lasted for a few seconds but Lilly knew that if she couldn't find her way up and out of the water she would drown. When she became aware of this reality her focus went to God and that if she died she would be with Him. What she describes as a peace that passes all understanding fell on her and all fear left. Her body went limp while this overwhelming peace filled her soul. The next moment she felt something stand her up and her head came out of the water. Marcos was commanded by God to intervene and help her get up out of the water. It was not her time to die. Lilly began to cry as she realized what happened to her. She had a sense of what dying might be like. The peace she felt and the memory of it never left her and to this present time, she still remembers it as if it happened yesterday. How close we come at times and we never realize that God sends His angels to help us more than we know. falon had nothing to do with this episode although he watched. This was just one of those freak situations that can happen because of the imperfect world we live in and the dangers that are out there. Lilly learned that day how quickly one's life can be swept away and how precious life really was. The peace that she felt when she thought her life was coming to an end made her know that even in death God would be with her and her outlook on dying changed. She no longer feared death and hated it. Lilly knew it was just a part of life and as we die God steps in and consumes us with His love and peace. From that one situation, she had matured in the knowledge of life and death and got a much clearer understanding of it. This settled her thinking on the subject and she was no longer in such rebellion over the cycle of life and death.

29

Death couldn't seem to touch Lilly because the Father God had placed a protective hedge around her to be set aside and mature into the woman he had purposed for her in life to be. falon began to hate her more and more as time went on and she progressed into womanhood. Her teenage years were behind her now and she had made it through without falling into any perverted traps he had set for her. A few boyfriends had come and gone and she still held her virtues. Her heart was still moved by humanity and life's hurts and sorrows but Lilly truly had no idea that the God of the universe had selected her to be a healer for the Glory of God. Her innermost instincts would always lead her towards the will to believe for life to go on in a positive way rather than accept defeat. Faith had been taught to her by her grandmother and although she didn't realize it was within her very being she did know that dear old Grammy's prayers were answered. She had seen many a time when Grammy had prayed earnestly for something the answer would come. Lilly did not know that her faith could also believe for results and see them manifest themselves. There was no love to her like her Grammy's love. Grammy just had that way of showing her the unconditional love of God. Lilly had a hard time accepting the love from God because she was so hard on herself. It was hard for her to believe that God could just love her the way she was. She was such a loving, caring child it seemed rather funny to see her always thinking the worst of her life. That same old insecurity kept her down. Marcos knew the time was coming when Lilly would see the light and begin to know the God who had sent His Son into this world so we could have fellowship with Him. falon also knew that she was becoming wiser with age and he wanted to stifle any move of the Spirit for her.

falon comes up with a plan and takes off into the lower chambers of darkness to speak his mind. he appears before the prince of darkness with his plan to break her heart and as he pleaded his case the plan was accepted. It was settled that a spirit of cancer would be sent to her earthly father to slowly destroy his body and eventually cause his death. Don't forget how Lilly hated death and had finally come to terms with this in her life. To have to watch her father who was only in his forties wither away from such a terrible disease was horrifying. falon thought it was great.

His plan would have to mess her up somehow he thought. Yes, the news was found out a few months later when her dad was diagnosed with cancer of the lymph glands and was given only six months to live. What a blow to this family. The timing could not have been worse because Lilly was engaged at this point with the wedding arrangements already made. The man who she was going to marry was not even the right person for her. They had been high school sweethearts but Lilly in her desperation to be loved was about to make a big mistake. Marcos knew it but he was not allowed to interfere in human decisions. The Holy Spirit was moving her spirit and trying to tell her he was not the one but she still was not spiritually aware enough to hear the voice of God yet. Not only was her father dying she was going into a marriage that was doomed to fail. Poor Lilly so full of love for her dad and yet there was nothing she could do. It was breaking her heart to see her dad this way. The cancer treatment had caused him to go bald. He would have to walk her down the aisle with no hair on his head. It didn't matter to Lilly but it was a bit embarrassing for her father. It was almost unbelievable for the family to accept this. The truth was they watched and they waited for the moment when it would be his time to go and be with God.

During this time period, The Holy Spirit was moving in on Lilly to accept the Lord as her savior. She had gone to church with her sister and when they asked for anyone who wanted prayer to come up front, something supernatural, blew her out of her seat. Lilly knew it was not from this realm. It was two angelic beings who grabbed her arms and literally pulled her up to her feet. The God of the universe had planned this day so an intervention was needed. She was walking up front feeling quite embarrassed because she had no idea why she was even going up. When it was her turn they asked her what should they pray about and Lilly just stood quietly. With no response from Lilly the Pastor just began to pray and Lilly got a zap from heaven and this language came out of her mouth that she had no idea about. The Pastor said that God was going to use this woman mightily. While the feeling was great during the prayer when Lilly walked away she also got hit with an extreme feeling of depression that made her feel terrible and confused. This was one of those sneaky, seeking whom they may devour demons who talk in your ear every chance they can when we lack knowledge. She knew both feelings were not of this world but had no idea what had happened to her. She had experienced what the word talks about when it says the enemy comes immediately to steal the seed that was planted. She had received The Holy Spirit and the devil got so angry that he sent a lying demon to tell her something different than what really happened. This supernatural experience was so overwhelming and Lilly had no idea what actually happened. She knew it was not of this world but that was all she knew. When she told her dad he told her she must have been hypnotized because he had no clue either about The Holy Spirit or the devil's attacks.

Lilly was touched by The Holy Spirit once again when she was alone in her room one night and she was telling God how much she loved him. She became so overwhelmed with her feelings of love for God she kept repeating it over and over again, "I love you, Lord, I love you, Lord." With those words, another language began to come out of her mouth and she got a bit nervous because she had no idea what it was. She was so moved by something she knew was not of this world. It was a power and a fire that seemed to consume her entire being. It was a feeling of peace and love and power and excitement. She got up and walked out of the room wondering what it was that had happened to her. She ran to her sister and asked her if she knew what happened and her sister told her it was The Holy Spirit. Lilly still did not understand but went back into her room and asked God to let it happen again. Nothing happened. Lilly was kind of alright with that because she had become so overwhelmed that she just took it for what her sister said. She did not have a life-changing moment then because she continued to live her life without any true knowledge of God or His Spirit.

She had another episode of the supernatural when her future husband and she ran into a few ex-drug addicts who had gotten saved and were sharing their testimony at the shopping center. They both sat down and listened and when it came time to be called up to accept the Lord a spirit flew across the parking lot and sat on her future husband's neck and began to speak loudly into his ear. He repeated word for word out of his mouth what was said to him by this being that looked like a gremlin. He leaned over towards Lilly and said in her ear, "if you go up it is all over between us." Lilly panicked and sat back down feeling very upset by what he had just said to her. They left and Lilly missed her chance to accept the Lord. Lilly had some idea now from hearing these men talk that she needed to make some kind of a decision to accept Jesus into her life. She had always believed He was the Lord but never had a real relationship with Him. Her prayers to God were usually praying He would not be mad at her for some of the things she had done. She lived a pretty decent lifestyle but was sexually involved with her future husband and felt very guilty about it. As far as Lilly was concerned she needed to marry him because he was the man she lost her virginity to and morally she had committed her life to him. The enemy was working overtime to keep this emerald-eyed beauty away from the truth about God including the man she was just about to marry.

Lilly got married and became pregnant right away. She was thrilled but her husband was not. Her hope was that her dad would live long enough to see his first grandchild be born. Grammy was cute because she thought Lilly had to get married when she found out she was pregnant. Back in her day, most women did not know so quickly that they were pregnant. With the modern technology, women find out so quickly. Lilly tried to explain to Grammy that she was only a few weeks pregnant but I don't think she ever got the right idea. Her dad was taking all kinds of experimental drugs and they were working rather well so the cancer was not progressing as fast as they thought. Lilly was living in the apartment upstairs from her grandmother after she had gotten married. The pregnancy kept Lilly focused on life rather than death and this really ticked falon off. He had such plans of devastating her emotions in this and it seemed it was not working. He had really thought the father was going to expire much faster than he was. The demons cannot understand that life is so precious to God and the human body was made to heal in many ways so even in a life threatening situation it can be harder than we think for our bodies to just stop living.

Over the years while Lilly was in the working scene before getting pregnant, this demon, who we are calling falon, did not stop his attempts to keep harassing her. There are so many situations I could write another book about them all but wanted to make it clear that along with blessings the devil is always out to

33

steal, kill and destroy in whatever way he thinks it will work. Since Lilly was quite beautiful to many onlookers, this was the main area the evil one felt he could make her fall. Lilly who was shy and very humble may I say, never once thought who she was, even though everywhere she went she had eyes on her all the time, so much so that she became quite uncomfortable with it. She would sit in restaurants and get stared at and wonder if it was just her imagination to keep thinking people were watching her. She could feel their souls as they looked. She knew what they were feeling. She did not like that people made such a big deal over her eyes. She gave all the glory to God for anything she had been given and never could understand why some people thought who they were because they were pretty when they did not create themselves. Why brag about something you did not even do. Brag on the one who made you that way. To recall some of the demonic attacks let me start with her first job. Her supervisor was an outright pervert and the demon was so obvious to her it disgusted her to have to work with him every day. During a Christmas party, he followed her downstairs into the file room and pushed her against the cabinet and began kissing her. Lilly wanted to get sick as she told him to stop and left the area. He actually called her on the phones in the office with harassing words like I am going to get you after work today! Lilly had enough and confronted the other boss and told her and he stopped. I guess he was threatened with getting fired. Then they hired a man who tried to get her to go into prostitution for him. This all comes with beauty even if you do not ask for it, it will follow you as it did poor Lilly. You see pervert demons act out through people so if you get involved with any kind of ungodly things the demons are just waiting for you to get their thrills too. Not exactly what God desires for His creation. Lilly did not have too many jobs because she was a stay home mom but every job she did have she dealt with sexual harassment. While she was a school crossing guard, a policeman stopped and asked her out and when she told him she was married he said, "so what". In another store where she worked, another manager who was twice her age asked her out and kept bothering her so she had to report him too so he would stop. How disgusting she thought as some of these men were old enough to be her father and who do they think they are. She could actually see the demons operating from these people and could feel the sickly desire they had because of these spiritual beings. In this same store, a man who was married to her sister in law came on to her too and she thought, "are you kidding me." It was so bad she could hardly believe it herself. At that time, she had no real knowledge of the spiritual realm but could feel the presence of these beings anyway. She never really understood how she could know what people were feeling. She just knew! falon really was relentless in his quest to bring her down or make her fall into some situation that would really break her up inside.

Men who were family members of her husband at this time were flirting with her in hopes she would respond. Men who worked with her husband as volunteer firemen made moves on her. One evening, after Lilly came out of the prayer group she attended, a man who was almost twice her age was sitting in his car waiting for her to come out. Lilly knew him from the fire department as one of her husband's friends. Lilly remembered a conversation he had with her husband when he told him, "someone is going to come along and take her away from you if you do not start treating her the right way." The day when Lilly heard him say this she had to hold back the tears because the marriage was not good and Lilly was so lonely and felt so rejected that she was very unhappy. This was the very man who was sitting in his car outside the church. Lilly saw him and was surprised he was there. He waved for her to come over to the car and told her to get in. This was a person Lilly knew so she got in the seat.

Now let me show you from the spiritual side what was happening. falon, the pervert demon had been watching this man for months. He heard conversations of how beautiful he thought Lilly was and how he wished he would be married to her. He could see that he thought Lilly's husband was a fool for ignoring her and he had the attitude he would give her what she desired. He was the perfect choice for falon to grab hold of. Lust was right up his ally and desperate Lilly, in need of love, was the perfect victim to step in for the kill. It would be even more perfect because now Lilly has the Lord in her life so what a greater trophy to make her fall right on her face. falon went after this guy will all the charm he could muster up and all the lustful desires he could instill upon this man's soul. falon knew he had to keep it cool and slowly move

35

in to take her out. The entire conversation was actually spoken by this demon and this is what he said, "How are you doing Lilly? I know you have had a rough time in your marriage. I think you need to have someone to talk to so you can deal with your life. You sit home by yourself every day and it's time for you to have some fun in your life. I will meet you tomorrow and we can go to the beach and talk so you can get out of the house for a bit." The demon made it like a friendship deal and Lilly was so desperately lonely at this point that it sounded good to her. She trusted this man and even though she felt some guilt in her soul she did not care because she had so many hurt feelings from her husband that when he told her she deserved to have a life she agreed. What a real smooth talker this demon, named falon was. Lilly knew in her spirit something was not right but what harm could it do to get out of the house for a bit and talk to a friend. The demon spoke to Lilly about how slighted she was by her husband and how unfair it was and this demon had it all down what he knew Lilly needed to hear to convince her to go. Lilly actually felt special after speaking with this man because he spoke with such sincerity that Lilly truly felt cared about for the first time in a long time. It sure was an angel of light just like the bible tells us. He was charming, seductive, seeming to care and acknowledging the feelings that Lilly was having. Lilly was extremely nervous but she was so bored and rejected that this was a thrill to actually get out of the house and go somewhere and be able to vent out her feelings.

They met and went to the beach. Lilly shared all of her hurts and the man listened which really impressed Lilly. He really seemed like he was genuinely concerned for her feelings. falon makes his move as he influences the man to kiss Lilly. With a lie from the pits of hell falon says in the man's ear, "she wants you so badly you have to make a move now while you have the chance. She needs a real man just like you to give her just what she needs. You're the man who can do it." Lilly felt moved by the kiss only because he seemed so sincere but as he took his hand and placed it upon her breast and began to lift up her blouse Lilly grabbed his arm. She looked right at him and point blank said, "I can have sex anytime I want to, that is not what I am looking for." The man told her how much he cared about her and how he had these feelings for years. "How flattering." Lilly thought. There was no

36

way she was falling into this sex thing. Her self-esteem was knocked down but one factor the demon did not account for and that was the power of God which was with Lilly. The man was obviously disappointed because his quest had failed. Let's say the demon was really ticked off at this point. He was trying to control his anger at her unwillingness to respond to his advances. Lilly told him it was time to leave and they got back in the car and drove home. Lilly was now very skeptical of this man's real intentions and her eyes suddenly opened in the spirit realm and she knew that he had a demon who was trying to take advantage of her. Her heart felt sick when she could see his annoyance at her. There was no real caring about her the way he had shown her from the start. He was angry but he still was not going to give up just yet. He told her he would take her for a trip to Paris the next day if she wanted. Lilly was truly tempted to go but the closer they got to her car the more obvious the demon became. falon was really ticked off. He wanted to blow up at her but had to really use his self-control so he wouldn't reveal his real feelings which were hate and envy. He was hateful at her decency to not fall into temptation. falon's pride was messed up and he knew he would be attacked by all the other demons when they found out that Lilly snubbed him. Lilly had the power of the Holy Spirit on her side and He, the Spirit, was not going to let this demon use her. Lilly really thought he cared and when she saw him for what he really was she was sick inside. He was no different than any other man who wanted her only for sex. Was there any man who was not full of himself and his need to just use women? Lilly ended this right then and there when she told him she wanted her marriage to work and not to call her anymore. The attention was really nice Lilly thought but what good was it when it was only for one purpose which was to have sex with her and probably dump her once he got what he wanted. "No thank you," Lilly thought to herself. The Holy Spirit let her see right through this pervert demon and Lilly was so thankful she did not fall prey to this man's intentions. She was hurt and sorrowful for even going to the beach that day but learned another lesson in life about the evil intentions of those who seek after their own lustful desires. Lilly realized what a sick world we live in. All she wanted was to be loved and it just seemed that was nowhere to be found.

Lilly had no rest when it came to men seeking her out and it did not change even after she got married. When men were around her it just seemed they would lose control and do things that were unbelievable to Lilly. Most of the men who knew her husband were the ones who did things behind his back and it would take Lilly by surprise all the time. Do not want to make this book into some sexual story so we will leave it at that but Lilly was definitely on the radar for demons to attack and all because she was considered pretty. The lustful spirits in this world are sickening and it really does take over the lives of many people who are ignorant to its tactics. There is a very real difference between lust and love and we need to realize that just some casual sex for your fleshly pleasure goes much deeper than you think. As spiritual beings, God made the sexual act holy and a bond between a husband and a wife and their souls merge together not just the body. Every person you have ever had sex with your soul merged with them and it will leave a scar if you do not pray for the soul connection to be broken. Sexual promiscuity was never meant to be and it has really screwed up mankind. Later on, in this book I tell about the book of Enoch and how the devil used his angels to reproduce with the women and beings were created that were half man and half angel. There are myths about it because it was true. Before the world was destroyed by water during the day of Noah these demonic angels disobeyed the rules and the devil began a creation of his own beings. These beings that are part man and angel all died from the flood but their spirits are still roaming around planet earth with nowhere to go. They are looking for people to attach to and fulfill their desires. The bible mentions these created beings so this is not something I am making up. Lilly has been a target her whole life for these angelic beings to come and try to lead her to the other side. While her life was moving on Lilly did get saved by realizing Jesus was her Lord. The Holy Spirit began to reveal himself a little bit at a time as situations would happen and Lilly had no answers accept that God had stepped in and did something supernatural.

Lilly was upstairs cleaning her house when she heard her grandmother cry out to her for help. She ran as fast as she could down the stairs and into the sitting room where she was. Grammy looked at her and said I'm going to die something is wrong with me. "I am having a heart attack," she said. Lilly was speechless. What could she do? She reached out to Grammy with her compassion and prayed for her. Lilly opened her mouth and said, "Grammy you are not going to die in the name of Jesus." With those words and I wish Lilly was able to see this but she was not ready yet, a most beautiful angel ascended from the heavens right into the room where they were both sitting. The angel was dressed in a beautiful white robe that shined from the glory of heaven. With a smile on his face and the peace of God permeating from his very being he stood in front of Grammy and placed his hand upon her heart. There was a sudden burst of light from the area where he touched her and it was as if what was happening to the heart just stopped. Truth be told what was happening to Grammy stopped immediately as she asked Jesus to help her. Unknown to Lilly at that moment her life was spared because of that prayer. She told her Grammy that she could not die yet because she had to be here when the baby was born. Lilly was about five months pregnant by now. Grammy lived for another few months feeling fine and you would have never known anything had happened that day. Beautiful Grammy about two months later was walking to town and had a heart attack and died. Lilly was at work when the news came through and was very upset. This was the first family member to die and would be her first funeral. Everyone had thought dad would be the first to go but it was the mercy of God to take dear Grammy home first. Grammy could not have watched her son die. This would have been too much for her so the timing was right for her to go and be with God. What upset Lilly was that she was bringing life into the world and here was a life leaving it.

This would have been Grammy's first great grandchild and Lilly was so sad she was not here to see this wonderful blessing. Lilly thought to herself, "was this a coincidence that she was bringing a life into the world and here was one that had just left. All the faith that Lilly had in Grammy's prayers were now gone. She would have to learn that her own prayers were just as powerful. It took a while for her to realize that the day she prayed for Grammy she was having a heart attack and because of prayer, Grammy did not die right then and there. The anointing of God was in her life but Lilly did not know of this healing power. It was an awesome thing too because every time Lilly got pregnant one of the grand-parents would die while she was pregnant. So Grammy was gone, the one who influenced her so much in the ways of the Spirit. Her poor grandfather was so lost without her. Lilly who lived upstairs helped grandpa. She couldn't leave the house without him calling her. It became rather annoying to Lilly but she showed him nothing but patience.

Lilly finally had her baby and it was a boy. The marriage stunk but Lilly was thrilled with her new son. Her dad was still here to see this blessing. It was a thrill for him because he had three girls and no sons. Lilly lived with each Christmas feeling it would be his last one and yet he kept making it. He was a strong man and although Lilly did not know it God has the complete say in when we are born and when we die.

Lilly and her husband and her son went on a vacation for few days. When they arrived her son was flushed in his face. Lilly had brought a thermometer and sure enough, he was sick with a fever. Lilly went into freak out mode. What was she going to do now with her sick son? She had been learning from watching some television shows that God was a healer. Even in today's world, she had heard that God did heal people. Lilly had no knowledge of the word of God at all. Grammy was no longer with them and she was the one who had all this faith to believe. Lilly was on her own now. She cried out to God and asked Him if He would heal her son. She talked with Him as if He was right there listening to her. She said she was sorry she did not know if He would do it or not but she really wanted to know the truth. If He did heal people in the world today she asked if He would show her by healing her son. She cried and cried to God for help and would He please have mercy on her ignorance and her son who was sick. Lilly was so upset in her soul. She barely slept at all as she continued to pray for healing if it were the will of God. It had to be the mercy of God because He heard her cries for help and her son was fine the next day. No fever, no nothing. Lilly had just had a lesson about healing. Again Lilly missed the beautiful angel of the Lord when he came to bring healing to her son. This time, the angel not only touched her son, releasing the power of God, he walked right over to Lilly and whispered into her ear. The words of encouragement were, "Lilly you have been chosen by God to bring His love to the world. Go in peace and fulfill your mission on earth with all the joy the Lord has to offer you." Lilly had no idea what he had said.

When Lilly was pregnant with her son she fell down her mother's stairs and sprained her ankle and her lower back now had a bit of an issue because when she fell the weight of the baby threw her lower disk off a bit. She went to a chiropractor for help because of how she was feeling. She was having allergies and her emotions were not good. She was not happy in her marriage and Lilly did not know but stress and emotions set off many of the physical conditions humans deal with. Rejection is a major factor in uneasiness of the soul which can cause allergies. Her husband in his cold heart would make fun of her and tell her it's all in your head. Maybe it was but she felt sick. At one of the visits, there was a nun who came just to pray for her. Lilly was embarrassed. Before the nun walked in the room Lilly began to cry and feel so sad and wondered what was going on. The nun came in and she tried to hide her emotions. The nun said, "you feel sad." Lilly looked at her and got a bit offended by this statement from a person who did not even know her. Lilly had no idea of the gifts of the Spirit at this time. With that remark, Lilly began to cry and started to tell the nun a story from when she was a baby. Lilly was in awe at what she was telling the nun because she had no idea what was really going on. She continued to tell the nun that when she was a baby she was left to cry for a long time and felt very rejected and unloved and she still felt that way. She felt like nobody loved her. The nun prayed and told her that she had gotten healed by God. Lilly felt no different. The nun then told her you will notice a difference in yourself. Just go about your life and one of these days soon you will see a change in how you feel about the love of God. Lilly left and had no clue what had just happened but a week or two later Lilly realized she did not feel unloved anymore. She knew without a doubt that God loved her and nothing else really mattered accept His love for her. She stopped feeling rejected and had entered into a truth about the love of Jesus. She had not realized that she was being filled with God. She knew she was different. What she did not see during the prayer for healing was that negative seed that was spoken to her by the demon when she was a child was removed. The power of the prayer made the lie leave her soul and get filled with the truth. They look like dark circles which are the fiery darts of the devil and they just pop out of our soul and are replaced with the light of God which is the truth. The same light that the angel touched her grandmother with was now given to her. It is the light of the healing power of God Almighty. Lilly was free from this feeling of nobody loves me and this truth became her strength and Lilly touched many lives with the same truth that set her free.

3. Two Kingdoms with Two Very Different Purposes

Years went by and Lilly had her second child which was a girl. During that time her grandfather passed away making her wonder again about life and death. It was now time for Lilly to step into the Kingdom of God and begin using her gifts for the Lord! What pushed Lilly into the Kingdom of God was right before her daughter was born she was having false labor. It got so intense Lilly got fearful. She noticed the bible on the shelf that had never been opened. It was a gift from her sister years before but Lilly, even though baptized by the Holy Spirit, had no idea. Nobody really took her to the side and explained the supernatural experience she had with the Spirit so she just continued to live life like everyone else was. She would go out to the bars with her husband on weekends and have fun. The men would be glaring at her with their lustful thoughts and Lilly could see the spirits. Lust and love are so opposite but Lilly had not learned enough to know the real difference yet. Attention was attention as far as she was concerned and she was desperate in her need for some attention. She got none from her husband. The marriage was doomed to fail because Lilly was not in love with this man. She was young and was looking for true love and fell into the trap of sex before marriage. I call it a trap because the focus is on the sexual relationship rather than the spiritual one. Lilly was not happy with this man and he had his own important things to do and they did not include Lilly. Lilly was just one of millions who marry for all the wrong reasons. Here she was having her second child and was just miserable in the relationship. She felt very rejected and unloved by him. It was what it was and Lilly was now focused on having this child. While she was waiting to go into real labor Lilly picked up this bible and flipped it open. She opened up to the chapter of Acts. Lilly began to read about the Holy Spirit falling on them and they all spoke with other languages. Lilly stopped dead in her tracks and it was as if a light went on in her head and she saw as clear as could be, the truth. She excitedly spoke out loud with nobody even in the room, "I have this Holy Spirit!" She knew from the scriptures that this language she had gotten years before was the Holy Spirit. Since the Holy Spirit was the third person of the Trinity she knew it was a good thing to have. With no knowledge of the word, Lilly was on fire. She went into labor right after that and had her baby girl.

After Lilly recuperated from the birth she had to find a place where she could go and be with other people who also had this Holy Spirit. She joined a prayer group and from the moment she joined the demons did nothing but make fun of her by using her husband and his friends. She dealt with it, knowing it went with the territory of persecution. Her father went into the hospital and it seemed that it was his time to go home. Lilly believed in miracles and still had this thing about death so she kept praying for healing. The day he died her mother called from the hospital and asked if Lilly and her sisters would pray for God to take him home because she was exhausted from staying there night and day just waiting for it to happen. She and her sisters all knelt down and Lilly asked God to either heal him or take him home. Right after the prayer was prayed he died. Lilly was amazed that the prayer was said and the answer came so quickly. It made her wonder about death and about the quick response. Her father was now gone and she wanted to know that he had made it into heaven. She had two dreams that night. One of him singing How Great Thou Art while being resurrected from the grave and the other was him telling Lilly to reach out to her mother with the truth about salvation. Lilly never forgot those dreams and the day did come when she had the opportunity to tell her mom about salvation.

Lilly made one vital mistake at this time in her life that would create demonic influence for many years to come and she had no clue about it. We can be influenced by these beings even as Christians and never know why we may feel one way or the other. We most of the time think it is us when in fact it is one of those creepy beings just busting our chops as one would say. Her husband was a fireman so they would have fire department dinners and there was always entertainment. This particular year they had a hypnotist, and everyone thought, how cool is that? Nobody really believed it worked. Lilly and her friends all went up to play the game. He made them do things that they would never have done on their own so it was pretty clear he was the real deal.

He seemed to stay away from Lilly and only did one thing with her. She walked up to him and felt an uneasiness from the start. Here go the demons in action! The man who had many spirits hanging around him looked into her eyes and told her she was going to see his eye looking like a cat's eye. She thought in her mind that nothing was going to happen. He touched the side of her neck and without Lilly even having a clue a spirit latched on and grabbed her shoulder. He told her to look at his eye and sure enough, she saw the eyes look just like a cat's eye. Lilly with her green eyes looked right back at him and he and his demon friends were so uneasy around Lilly that he ushered her away and did the main focus on the other people. After this episode, Lilly had some problems with her neck and back where it would just twitch for no reason and she just ignored it. The tension was mounting in her neck from this spirit and for many years she had no idea until she grew to the spiritual level where it was revealed and rebuked. Entering the dark side with fortune tellers and hypnotists and anything else we are told to stay away from can bring upon us all kinds of issues. Even if we have no understanding of it, we still can be harassed by demons because we open up to it. This particular demon we will deal with later on in the story but it made a home right there on her neck creating discomfort for her. It also had its own personality that Lilly had to deal with. All the feelings this being had would now be pushing itself on Lilly. She had her own sweet soul but had to now deal with this evil spirit's personality. It was here to stay and was thrilled to be part of tormenting a child of God. That would be kudos for the demons. To grab hold of the Christians who do not have a clue where the enemy can actually hang around them was the ultimate feeling of pride for them. Lilly could actually feel a physical discomfort on her shoulder because of this spirit. Unbelievable isn't it? How dare they do what they do. We seem to think of movies like the Exorcist when dealing with demons. They can totally control someone but that is only when The Holy Spirit is missing and the person walks into the kingdom of darkness. That is possession. Christians who deal with demons are only oppressed or obsessed. One is the spirit hangs around the outside and influences and the other is when a Christian lives in some sort of sin and becomes obsessed with it. That allows the demon to begin controlling the mind and the thought patterns we have and they can be from the spirit itself. When a demon influences your mind you will have a hard time resisting it. It will be relentless in its torment and will basically push you to do what it wants you to do. They have no real power over us unless we let them in. Ignorance is one of the main reasons they come into our lives. We just do not know any better and then we think it is our personality when in fact it is the demons. Lilly was not possessed she was being oppressed. In other words, she would be able to feel its personality at times and her body would feel the stress the demon was creating on it. Our feelings should only be our own personality and the influence of The Holy Spirit. The battle of the minds was now on as Lilly had to follow the Holy Spirit rather than her negative thoughts at times. We all deal with this but it becomes a bit harder when a spirit is involved in influencing people.

Lilly was now learning about The Holy Spirit and that there were gifts given. She was so on fire for God that she could not put the bible down. She witnessed a few things during this time in her life that she would never forget. It was the beginning of her anointing really surfacing. Lilly was walking around the apartment she lived in and felt moved to go look out the window. There was a woman walking through the parking lot next to the house and she was drunk and staggering everywhere. She was known as one of the town drunks. The Spirit moved her to rebuke the demon and she said from upstairs where the woman could not hear, "I rebuke you, alcoholic demon, in the name of Jesus." As she said those words the woman literally spun around and almost fell to the ground. It was obvious that something hit her with a force and made her spin. She continued to walk through the parking lot and Lilly never saw her again. Rumor had it that she stopped drinking and Lilly was the only one who knew what had actually happened. God had delivered her without her ever knowing what hit her. That is love and compassion.

A few weeks went by and Lilly gets moved again to look out the window. She sees a man getting out of his car with a wheelchair. The Holy Spirit tells her to go down and tell him about Jesus. Lilly gets upset because she was so shy she did not want to do it. She thought by the time I get down there he will be gone anyway. Maybe she was just talking to herself and it was not the Holy Spirit she thought. She needed to know if it was God before she would make a fool of herself and go witness to this man who would probably reject her. The Holy Spirit said, "he'll be back." She felt terrible and said she was sorry. A week went by and Lilly felt to go over to the window again. He was back getting his wheelchair out. Lilly got convicted as the Holy Spirit told her to go tell him about the Lord again. She died on the spot because she was so insecure she could not bring herself to do it, again. She was so grieved in her soul and asked the Holy Spirit to please help her overcome this insecurity. She prayed that He would zap her when He wanted her to do something for Him. She was so shy back then that although she wanted to be obedient she was bound by this force that compelled her not to react and do anything that would make her feel uncomfortable. Lilly had no idea it was one of those imps. Just when the Holy Spirit would speak this ugly being would push himself on her. Let me explain what happened in the spiritual realm. The light of the Lord flamed her spirit and soul with the fire to share the truth. It ignited her soul and she was being moved to act upon it. Immediately as this seed was planted in her soul the demon steps in and quenches the fire with his negative feeling of fear and embarrassment that would occur if she did what she was being told to do. The feeling of panic engulfed her and she was almost paralyzed. A battle was going on between her flesh and her spirit as two real beings from the spiritual world were influencing her. She could feel them both tugging at her. She wanted to obey the Spirit of God but the reason the other feeling won out was because she was more interested in listening to the flesh rather than her spirit at that time. She had a choice but chose to allow the negative feeling to override the other. She did not really want to feel embarrassed. We can override many of the feelings we get but most of the time we just accept them. To be honest, Lilly did not want to go and talk to this man. She let the demon win. She did not do it on purpose but she was lacking the knowledge she needed to take authority over it. She felt terrible and guilty at the same time. This is the war all humans face daily. The war between the spirit and the flesh. Lilly was learning and knew she needed help. She was humble enough to ask the Father to zap her or make her do it. God does not make us do anything but Lilly specifically asked

Him to make sure she did not miss anything He wanted her to do for Him. Marcos was also there to help inspire Lilly when things got spiritually heavy. With this second time of missing the mark Lilly heard as clear as day, "he'll be back." She died again on the inside. She would have to deal with this again. Every time she heard the words," he'll be back," she could feel the Father smiling as He was pushing her to respond to Him not the flesh side of her. She knew He was not mad and she definitely had been healed of feeling rejected by Him. If this would have happened years ago before that sweet little nun prayed for her she would have thought God was going to strike her down with lightning or something. Her idea of God from her church background was that God was this strict task master who you better obey or else. God is just and the judge but slow to anger. His patience goes way beyond what we would ever tolerate as human beings. He loved Lilly and was showing Lilly how to get free from the evil we deal with while on earth. Lilly was maturing slowly but surely. Lilly was outside, a few weeks later and the Holy Spirit tells her to turn around. "Oh! No," she thought. He was back. This time, she was outside and he was only a few feet away from her as he pulled into the parking lot that bordered the house she lived in. She died within her soul because she knew what she had to do. The Holy Spirit said, "go and tell him about Jesus." She tried to get her friend who was with her to go and tell him but her friend told her the Lord asked you to do it. Lilly was trying to get out of it again because of this overwhelming fear. She also knew that maybe three strikes and she would be out. She did not want to push the patience and mercy of God in this. She took a deep breath and emotionally rebuked the negative feelings and walked very quickly around to the front to get out of the fenced in yard. She thought about what she was going to say to this stranger who was getting his wheelchair out again. She felt sick inside from fear but kept on walking towards him feeling so humiliated already. The demon was putting the pressure on and Lilly felt like she wanted to pass out from the stress. As she got closer to him she could feel a difference as the Holy Spirit began to override her flesh. She boldly told the man that Jesus loved him and she told him a church she felt he would like to maybe go to. He looked at her like she was nuts but she smiled and said have a good day and left. She did it! Thank the Lord she had finally obeyed what the Lord wanted her to do. She overcame her fear and chose to follow what God was telling her rather than the influence of the evil one. Mr. imp flew away as he got his rear end kicked with faith and trust and obedience. She found it much easier after this episode to obey God. She was still battling with shyness but this was one step closer to freedom. She felt great even though she felt the guy thought she was crazy.

There was a man who was known in the town that Lilly lived in as a drunk and a troublemaker. He lived a few blocks away from Lilly and he had gone to school with her so she knew all about him. One night Lilly had gone to sleep and got woken up with a sound coming from the parking lot next to the apartment she lived in. It was a moaning sound as if someone was hurt. Lilly stayed in bed listening and feeling very nervous about this. She called her mom who lived downstairs at the time and she had called the police. Lilly just sat in bed and listened to these ungodly sounds coming from this person. She knew there were demons tormenting this person by the way he was moaning. Yes, the demons were all over him in the drunken stupor he was in. They had knocked him to the ground and were screaming in his ear all kinds of obscenities and he was feeling like he was going to die. The demons were having a field day as they jumped all over his back and screamed out, "we got another one and we will take him out. Not much longer and we will receive our trophy for sucking the life out of his spirit. What a loser you are and this one is one of the worst losers on planet earth. He hasn't enough brains to stay out of trouble. He listens to everything we tell him. Aha! Aha! we are winning on planet earth. Our lord satan will reign and we will bow down before him on his thrown on the earth. Not much longer before the man chosen to be possessed by our satan will be taken over and we can really be free to destroy many of these disgusting human beings. Can you imagine God creating them in His image and likeness and we just get screwed? After we finish this creep off we will find another fool to devour." He then vomited all over himself and he just was sprawled out on the ground like a wounded animal. The demons were seeking to kill him that day, but something happened that was so amazing, and Lilly heard it audibly from her bedroom. Lilly did not see this but an angel of the Lord appeared next to this lost soul right in the midst of his filthiness and began speaking words of inspiration to him. The angel so full of joy smiled as he looked down at what looked like a lifeless figure of a man. With all the glory of God, the angel shined a ray of hope that penetrated into the lost soul of this man and then Lilly heard something that made her weep in anguish for his soul. The angel motivated him and also moved Lilly to pray a prayer of deliverance for him. Lilly heard these words resonate from the parking lot below her window, "God help me, God please help me I cannot take this anymore." He was pleading with God to help him and it was coming from his inner being, his spirit. It was so heart wrenching that Lilly burst into tears as he repeated the words over and over again in such agony of soul. Lilly had never heard anything like this and never ever did again after that day. Lilly being moved with such emotion, listening to his plea for help from God, screamed out from her bed to the God of the universe to do something to help him. Lilly could feel his anguish of soul and yelled as loud as she could, "God do you not hear him? He is asking you to help him. You have to help him, Lord, he is begging you to help." Lilly was crying and pleading with God to help him too as he continued to cry for help. It was almost more than Lilly could handle and she was thankful when the police arrived because she figured they would help him. When they saw who the person was they just kicked his foot with their shoe and said, "It's only Sam." and they left. Lilly was in shock that they just left him there like an animal and she cried all the more begging God to help him. Things got quiet and he finally got up and walked away. Lilly was quite upset over the whole experience and never forgot it. Lilly knew nothing of what happened to him after that until some years later when he actually walked into her church. Lilly was stunned because he was the last person you would ever think would walk into any church. He knew Lilly and Lilly knew him so she walked over to him and asked him how he was doing and he smiled and told her he got saved. Lilly was so overwhelmed and she knew God had heard both their cries that day and did answer. What an awesome God we have! The demons fled in terror that day as the angel of the Lord stood before them and Lilly prayed the prayer for him to be delivered and set free. This very same man before coming to the Lord got another man's wife pregnant and Lilly just so happened to run into her as she was walking down the street. She was supposed to be a Christian but was married and had this man's child in her womb and did not know what to do. Lilly was sent by God that day because she was on her way to have an abortion. She told Lilly that Christians were telling her to abort the baby and she did not know what to do. Lilly told her it was murder and she agreed. Lilly told her to give the baby up for adoption if she could not keep it but God would help her if she trusted him and did not kill it. She accepted the counsel of Lilly that day and had the baby and her husband accepted her and the baby regardless of what she had done. He knew the marriage was in trouble and he was part of the problem so he had forgiveness and a life was saved. Our steps are divinely ordered and this day proves it. She was on her way to have the abortion done when Lilly just happened to pass her by and stop to say hello. Lilly had no idea what she was about to do but God did. Again I will say, "what an awesome God we serve."

Things took a turn for the worst in the marriage after Lilly started walking with the Lord. The division was too much and the lack of love in the marriage drove Lilly into the arms of a Christian man who she truly fell in love with. He was also part of the prayer group that Lilly had joined. Prayer partners were chosen and Lilly was put with him as her prayer partner not knowing that she was going to actually fall in love with him. She was not quite sure about this man when she first met him because something unbelievable happened to him and Lilly thought he was either the biggest liar she had ever met or he was anointed by God. She knew he had some emotional issues too because he had a lot of fear that she could see. They became friends and Lilly prayed for him all the time because she knew the devil was out to get him. Lilly would never have looked to fall in love and break up her marriage but what happened with her emotions was out of her control. The love was so strong that Lilly could not resist it. The guilt was there too but Lilly after being rejected and ignored for so many years just did not want to walk away from true love. Lilly was a faithful wife and had many opportunities to cheat during the marriage but never would have. This was different because falling in love with this man came out of nowhere. Lilly had been

51

having a dream for weeks about meeting a man that she would fall in love with and what she would do about it. The dream was very real when she had it and she really wondered what she would do if it ever really happened. It did happen and Lilly was caught in the reality of what to do.

This part of the story is what propels the life of Lilly and this man into ministry together. His name will be David in this book and one day David was reading a scripture about the Holy Spirit in Ezekiel and saw a piece of newspaper floating in the water. He noticed it because the word GOD was shining from the water in large letters. He went and got the wet paper out and the exact scripture he was reading was in the article also about the Holy Spirit that was floating in the water. He was stunned by this amazing thing that happened to him. The article also had a part about Noah's Ark in it where the wrath of God has come down upon the earth. He kept this close to his heart because it was not a coincidence he was reading this exact scripture and then here this paper is floating on the water about Noah's Ark and the sprinkling of clean water upon the children of God. It was about the Holy Spirit coming upon them. When he showed this newspaper to Lilly she was in awe. This man was obviously chosen by God or he was a real liar. Lilly prayed about it because it frightened her. If he had made it up that would be terrible and if it was true he was truly called of God to do something for Him. Lilly still had no idea she was chosen too. This article and a vision about a place where Christians would live together were the motivating factors in the ministry that Lilly and this man started. Lilly fell so in love she had no control. The paper was truly sent by God and they both had a destiny to be together even in the midst of the sin. God would use this for His Glory.

Divorce and guilt followed but it was true love and the man was an anointed believer just like she was. The whole situation with what happened with Lilly and David is another story in the book called "Maybe Tomorrow," written by Lilly. While her life was in limbo and she was by herself with her two children she would pray and just trust God in her feeling guilty over what had happened. Once again we come into a situation where sin takes place and the door is opened to the demonic. Guilt too can become a spiritual battle we live with. Plenty of these beings going around seeking whom they may devour. It does not mean you have to have a being from the spiritual realm trying to control your life but if it is a feeling you cannot get rid of you probably are being influenced by one. You might say at this point how can we avoid these attacks when we have no clue about them. That is the problem, we have no clue. You can think you live a good life and a decent life and yet these fallen angels need a body to access so they can function and fulfill their desires. Whatever their desire is. Whatever you can think of in a negative way there are demons that fit. Remember one thing the devil is out to get the children of God. They are the people he wants to bring down. The world already follows him. The innocent children of God are the ones he wants to destroy. If you think you are a Christian and the devil cannot touch you, you better think about it for a minute. If you stay out of his territory, he can only get so close. If you like Lilly dabbles in his area you just opened the door for him. Lilly has now done several things wrong and is paying the price for it. She still has not moved into the spiritual realm herself yet because she has no real knowledge of the word of God. falon has been watching closely and doing his best to send perversion her way. Too many times to tell he actually used people to try and bring her down. Sicko demons approached her too.

She had a man follow her around the mall one day just staring at her from a distance. Everywhere she went this guy was right behind her. She waited until the right moment and then turned around back at him and rebuked him in the name of Jesus. If you would have seen his face when she rebuked him. The demon that was molded into him fearfully ran away. All we see is the face of the person. You can see the reaction of the demon by the expression on the person's face. This man when rebuked opened his mouth wide open and his eyes looked like he had seen a ghost. He sure did, it was The Holy Ghost using Lilly to stop his lustful eyes. The demon did not leave his body because he liked his sin but the person had to leave. They both left together and Lilly was disgusted at this perverted spirit that was gawking at her and following her everywhere. This was her life. She was constantly being gazed upon by demons who would lustfully watch her. Lilly knew the difference between true love and lust. One was beautiful and the other was just gross. Why would anybody want to be taken advantage of and be used without the person really caring about them at all? It was beyond Lilly's understanding.

Lilly and David went to buy a pizza one day and Lilly was feeling so excited in The Spirit. She walked past these two men who were standing outside the pizza place and Lilly looked at them and said, "Jesus loves you." Make sure when you do anything you check it out with the Lord first. Lilly was coming out of her shyness and this was a really bold move on her part but just because one might feel zealous for the Lord it does not mean we should be shouting things out everywhere we go. There are times and places and people who we are supposed to minister to. The Lord knows the people we should be talking to and the ones we should not. If we just walk up to anybody this is what might happen. Lilly got the scare of her life this day. She never realized that you really have to be moved by The Spirit not just your own excitement in the flesh. The one man after she said, "Jesus," got an angry, full of hatred look on his face. He moved towards her and put his face in front of her face so close she wanted to die and said, "What did you say?" Lilly felt the attack right into her soul as she felt the anger shoot at her. She did not say another word but walked into the pizza place. The man had so much anger she was thankful he did not touch her. She learned a real lesson that day. Just because we feel happy about the Lord does not mean we tell just anyone. It has to be done in The Spirit with His leading and protection. There are demons out there who hate the children of God and this man had demons. Lilly felt them and could see it manifest in the man's face. She knew that the look he gave her was the demon combined with the man. It was so scary for Lilly that she cried when she got back into the car. Such evil. It should not be, but it was. She saw the face of the demon and the face of the man combined into the same expression. Demons morph into us and mold themselves into what we look like and depending on how bad off you are you will feel what they feel and be moved to do what they want you to do. The sin of man has brought these beings into our lives. If we walk with the Lord, they cannot control us but can attack when we are vulnerable. We have to resist the devil and he will flee the bible says. Lilly was so upset she had to go home and just sit in the presence of the Lord. She cried and cried. Marcos was on the alert and he was the one who stepped up and went back at the demon and caused him to stop before actually touching Lilly. Angels and demons confront each other when necessary. As the demon got closer to Lilly Marcos moved in front of her and looked at the demon. With the light from God shining from his being the demonic being got scared and backed up. Two forces of power. One stronger than the other.

Lilly has had so many encounters with demons and healings it is almost impossible to write them all down. A friend of theirs was diagnosed with cancer and he called for prayer. Lilly and her son prayed this day and her son told his mother that there was a spirit being sitting on his arm. Lilly knew her son was beginning to see some of these creatures. Kind of scary for a child but the Holy Spirit knows what He is doing. Lilly asked the man where the cancer was and sure enough, it was exactly where her son saw it. Lilly rebuked it in the name of Jesus. He went back to the doctor and it was gone. This man's wife had a bladder that had fallen and was in need of an operation. Prayer was made and the bladder went back into place and she was healed.

Her son hurt his leg after going sleigh riding one day and Lilly was in the hospital with him. Across the room was a poor little girl who was having a severe asthma attack. She was not in very good shape and Lilly had compassion on her from across the room. She was actually watching this spirit torment this child. It was glaring right at Lilly and it made her feel uncomfortable. It was causing this child to not be able to breathe as it overpowered her lungs and was creating all kinds of physical things to happen to her. The child was under such an attack that she was out of control. This thing was in full control. Righteous anger welled up in Lilly for what it was doing and it was so clear to Lilly but nobody else had an idea what was actually going on. They were treating the symptoms but the cause went beyond just the symptoms. It was a real live creature, a being from the other side and it was as real as you and I are. Lilly saw it so clear. Lilly very quietly told the demon to leave her in the name of Jesus and the child sat up and stared back at Lilly and with a loud ear piercing scream the demon yelled and flung her back on the bed making her wrench all over the place. The doctors all came running and Lilly freaked out herself because she did not expect that to happen from the simple prayer she prayed. She was just learning all these things about the spiritual realm and Lilly got a bit scared over the ordeal. Lilly still has no idea what happened to the child after the prayer and the whole screaming episode because she had to leave with her son. She prayed that God would have set her free. What do these beings look like? It is hard to say because some morph into the person's head, while some are just sitting on their shoulders and when it is an affliction it becomes part of whatever the problem is. Sounds crazy I know but ask Lilly because she has seen many over the years. Each one has a specific purpose and reason for being there and every time it is not good. The angels of God are also with us and they influence in a positive way. Words of inspiration and comfort for our souls as we go through this life of much trial and sorrow. This brings us to the next amazing supernatural thing that happened to Lilly!

Lilly felt moved to take her son to the beach one day to pray by the water. Her son was gifted too in the spiritual realm so they went to pray together. While they were sitting there in prayer, people with demons were walking by the car staring at the two of them. It was so obvious that these spirits were wondering what was going on. All at once Lilly felt to look up in the sky and she saw a line of angels standing in a row. She asked her son if he saw anything and he said he saw the same thing. Now we have a confirmation for what is going on. One angel stood out from the rest and Lilly knew it was coming down to give her something. Her son again saw the same thing. As the angel was heading down her son said: "mom the angel is coming down to give you something." She told him she knew because she could see it too. The angel stood by the car door and handed her a check for 2 million dollars in the spiritual realm. Her son saw this and Lilly held the check to her heart until the time it was meant to manifest in this natural realm. Lilly has still not yet seen this come to pass.

Here is another nice part of the story you will enjoy reading. One night Lilly was praying and she forgot to take off her glasses and fell asleep. She got woken up by a tapping on her forehead and as she looked across the room to her utter amazement there was an angel of God standing in the corner of the room as if he was guarding the house. For a few seconds Lilly could see his face, his wings and he did not look at her but was just hanging out up towards the ceiling. She was so thrilled to have seen one opened eyed like this. She saw this as if it was in the flesh realm. In other words, it was not in her mind it was right there. She quickly remembered the prayers her grandmother had always prayed for the protection of the house and Lilly figured he was there to protect the house. She would never forget this. Wow! A real angel of God. Distinct features too! Lilly still was not realizing this gift of God!

Lilly was starting to get dreams that would actually happen! One particular dream she had was a woman who had spirits and she came to a Christian club for prayer. Lilly in the dream was rebuking the demons and it was so real to her. A week later this very same woman who she saw in the dream showed up at this center and was in need of deliverance. This story is told in depth later on in the book. Another dream she had was of her mom coming home early with their fifth wheel while Lilly was allowing the man she fell in love with to stay in her apartment while she was gone. It's not something that she should have really done but at the time he was homeless and her mom was away. Three times in one month she had this dream where her mom got home early and caught him living in her apartment. The dream was so vivid it showed the truck pulling into the parking lot and then her mom walking in while Lilly was standing in the hallway of the apartment. Sure enough, the dream came to pass exactly as it was shown to her. It was possible that in the mercy of God he was trying to save her from the whole ordeal because she had compassion on him being homeless.

While Lilly was praying one day she saw Jesus standing before her and she fell to her knees. He told her to stand up and when she did he told her she was going to be ordained and if any man came against her he would openly show them she was called of God. I don't know about you but it sure seems to me that this emerald-eyed lady is most definably chosen by God. A few weeks later, sure enough, Lilly was ordained by a man that The Holy Spirit told to ordain her. You have not seen anything yet in what God does with her.

Cannot swear by this part of the story but did seem kind of suspicious. Lilly had to go to a place where she had some business to deal with and while she was waiting there was a man sitting next to her. She thought to herself that she might as well try to talk to him about the Lord and maybe get him saved so she started a conversation. To her surprise, he brought the conversation right to the bible. She was shocked but this was right up her ally so they began to talk about the word. The actual thing that happened was he started to basically preach to her about how true the word is. She sat in awe at his knowledge. She went into her meeting and walked out and he walked in as she left to leave. She went down the stairs into the lobby and when she turned around he was right behind her smiling. She looked at him and said, "How did you get here so fast?" He just smiled and she smiled back as if to say I see you and know who you are. She went to go and turned back to see where he was going and he was gone. He would have had to walk way across the room to leave but he was gone. They say there are angels in the flesh so this may have been one of them! All of these things happened during her first marriage and while she was waiting for her divorce.

The man who Lilly fell in love with, they did get married. The supernatural message from the sea that David had gotten and the vision of this place of peace and safety made them start a not for profit ministry of helps and teaching the word in a church atmosphere. Lilly's visitation from the Lord must have moved things in the spiritual realm because a few weeks later Lilly had gotten ordained and now both of them were ordained ministers. This is where Lilly really started to shine for the Lord. She was no longer hindered by a marriage with an unbeliever who the Lord tried to tell her was not meant to be in her life before she ever married him. She was thankful for her two beautiful children but the marriage should have never been. A mistake was made and people got hurt but God forgave Lilly and He does use all things for His glory. This does not excuse sin in any way but even when we fall the God of this universe knows and makes the way for us to recover and make things right. The Lord began to do some real miracles with Lilly. During church service in their backyard one day, the children after service were playing and must have gotten into some poison ivy. Yes, they got poison ivy and Lilly got so angry because here they were at church and got this. She walked to the back yard where she knew the poison ivy was and pointed her finger at it and commanded it to die in the name of Jesus! She walked away and went about her business. She came back later to do some praying and walked by the area where the poison ivy was and to her amazement, the poison ivy had withered up and died. She doubled checked the area to make sure it was the same place and her spirit rose up in excitement as she knew that it really did happen. The plants were actually dried up and were dead. She immediately thought of the scripture where Jesus curses the fig tree and it too withered up and died and the disciples were amazed. Here was Lilly amazed too and she knew she had spoken the words. What is this she thought? She knew it was The Holy Spirit but she also knew that this kind of thing is out of the ordinary!

While they lived in this house Lilly was praying one day and out of nowhere, she received a word from the Lord with a vision. It was as if God placed a desire within her heart of His will for her. He told her she was going to have another son and right then and there Lilly saw the face of this baby. For a person who did not want any more children, Lilly became quite excited about having another child. It was an immediate heart attitude change. The Lord spoke three things about this baby that was to come. He was going to have a heart for God, he was going to be strong in stature and he would be a lot like his father. Lilly did not know the challenge that would come along with this prophecy. She was beginning to see God move in miraculous ways with people she met and prayed for. There were women who came for prayer who could not get pregnant and after she prayed they got pregnant. This was not just a one-time thing it was every single time she prayed the women would be able to conceive. It was not as if she did anything either. It was a prayer in the name of Jesus and amen a child is conceived. She was personally excited about getting pregnant too but it became an issue when nothing was happening. She had children before and so did her husband but time went on with no child. Lilly petitioned the Lord about this because she was getting older and older and did not understand what the waiting was all about. Then there was the part where the enemy came in and tormented her about it. If it were not necessary to tell the whole truth it would be great to leave out all the imps who made it into this story. This one demonic being who we will call tormento hung around during this waiting period to try and steal this vision. He would relentlessly tell her she was getting old and she just had this thing about a baby because of it and God had not said anything about a son being born. None of it was real and she was never going to have another baby. It would get her so upset that she would cry. She knew in her soul that God had spoken to her but the waiting was trying to drive her crazy. It was not even her will to have another child so what was up with this constant harassment? Just one more evil thing to deal with. Lilly went to garage sales to find little things for the baby even though she was not pregnant. With the negative force coming at her she kept standing on what was truth. Truth to her was this baby was coming at some point in time. tormento was so full of jealousy towards the human race and their ability to reproduce that he was thrilled to have this task of pulling her down. By the way, falon never did succeed in taking her down with his perversion plans. All glory to God for that because there was plenty of perverts going around and looking to devour her. She even had them call her on the counseling line for people who needed prayer. Anyway, let's not go back to that and all the sicko demons out there.

During this time of waiting, two amazing things happened when Lilly prayed. The first situation was her husband's daughter was rushed to the hospital bleeding while she was pregnant. Lilly prayed to God and she got a knowing that the baby was going to be born that night and be alright! She told her husband as he ran out the door to the hospital. Sure enough, the word was from the Lord! One baby saved.

The other wonderful story was one of the women in the church who was pregnant and was supposed to be taking insulin but was not had a life and death incident. She called Lilly and told her she did not feel the baby move in days. She told Lilly that she felt the baby was dead. Lilly felt compassion for her but did not know if the baby was really dead or not. Lilly lifted her hands up to God while she was on the phone with the woman and asked God to bring the life back into the baby. As The Spirit took over and Lilly began to pray she knew that the baby was dead and it was one of those times when Lilly absolutely knew that God was going to do just that, bring the baby back to life. If you would have been there and would have seen what happened in the spiritual realm your life would never be the same again. Listen to

60

this it is unbelievable what God did. Lilly was blessed enough to see this and that is how this is being shared with the rest of us. An angelic being with its wings spread out was shining the glory of God with a light that was so brilliant it was almost hard to look at as it was coming down from heaven. Lilly could see the spirit of the unborn baby in its arms as the angel came to bring the life back to the baby that had died in the womb. She knew the child was alive once again after evil had sucked the life out. Lilly watched in her mind's eye a brilliant light beaming from the baby's chest as the angel placed the spirit back into the body. It was a brilliance that glowed and lit up the entire room as life was put back into the unborn baby. The baby was not born that day because it was too early and she left the hospital with the Glory of God shining from her womb. After seeing this miracle, the mom did not care when they told her the baby would not be normal when it was born. She did not believe that either and the baby boy was perfectly normal when his day came to enter this world. I have to add this part in because when the woman went to the hospital the baby was still dead. So what happened when Lilly prayed? She was shown what was going to happen as if it already had. The woman then went to the hospital and sure enough, they told her the baby was dead. She had a lot of faith and she told them her pastor had prayed and they needed to take the test again because the baby is not dead. They thought she was just a distressed mom but did it anyway to appease her. This went on for four times as she kept telling them to retake the test. Cannot remember for sure how many times they checked the heartbeat but it was a few and on the fourth time or fifth time they got a heartbeat. Yes, the baby was dead and came back to life with evidence to prove it. They also told her the baby would not be right from being dead so long but again were proven wrong by the power of God. Lilly was being used by God to bring life into the womb of women who could not have children and now bringing life back that was already dead. Lilly did not think twice about this because it was God who did it but she never in her humility accepted that she was chosen and anointed. How many people do you know who pray and people come back to life? We all know of Jesus with Lazarus but that was Jesus so we accept it. The Holy Spirit is no different in us than in Him so why not have an anointing to bring back life or give life where there is no life? The woman who had this baby also had a large tumor in her stomach before she had the baby. Lilly and David prayed and the tumor disappeared. Lilly was beginning to realize that feelings had nothing to do with healing. God did it whether you felt all this faith or not. It was the obedience in doing what He says to do that made it happen. It was the power in the name of Jesus that made everything happen. You didn't have to be feeling anything. There were times when Lilly prayed and had no knowing anything was going to happen and it just would happen right in front of her eyes. There were times when she would just know God was going to heal the person and He did. She learned that each situation was unique and God's will was going to be done. Lilly witnessed people ripping neck braces off their necks after being healed. She saw a woman receive her hearing back. People with back problems got healed. People needing inner healings had their lives changed after prayer. Demons were leaving people. Lilly and David were a team. The woman whose baby came back to life had a husband who got involved in listening to a man who was in a cult. He began to come against Lilly and David because of it even though they had been friends. He stopped coming to the church and began to harass them by throwing firecrackers outside the building while service was going on. It was very demonic and a bit scary. Lilly got up one morning and the Holy Spirit told her to fast for him to be delivered. Lilly obeyed the leading of the Lord and fasted and prayed for the day. That very same day at their evening service this man shows up after being away for months. Lilly was shocked but she knew she had fasted and was amazed at how fast something was happening with him. As service began and Lilly was playing the organ this man started to scream and the demon manifested right in front of the entire church. David walked towards him under the power of the Holy Spirit and placed his finger on the man's forehead. The man proceeded to act just like the Hulk and with all the power he had he tried to stand up. He was unable to move as the demon screamed in terror. The name of Jesus was used and the demon screamed its way out as he leaped to the floor. When he finally got quiet the man stood up and said he saw Jesus standing in front of him so he jumped to grab His feet and that was when the demon left. He said while

David had his finger placed on his forehead he tried with all of his might to get up and could not move. The power of God was so strong he just could not get up and punch David in the face which is what he wanted to do. It is what the demon actually wanted to do but could not. This all happened because Lilly had fasted for him and it opened the door for deliverance. Lilly was in awe at the power of fasting and praying.

One day they had only tuna fish for dinner and they prayed and thanked the Lord. They laughed and said it sure would be nice if this was lobster. With that, the phone rang. I mean the phone rang before they even started to eat and a brother said he had just gotten six lobsters and he hated lobsters so he thought of Lilly and David and wanted to give them to the family. Bring them right on over brother! Wow! That is not all the Lord did when it came to providing food. The refrigerator was empty a lot but none of them complained about it. Thinking about what to have for dinner when there is no food in the house is not easy. They decided that fish were free and they would go fishing for their dinner. They had only one fishing pole and no bait. They had a jar of olives so they grabbed the olives, the pole and they found a string that would be used with a hook they would put on the end. When they arrived at the dock they all stood in front of it and raised their hands and said these exact words, "fish bite these lines in the name of Jesus." Lilly and her daughter took the string after that simple command that was spoken and slowly let it sink under the water right off the side of the dock. As the line was going down they both watched thinking what could they possibly catch with a simple hook and string and believe it or not an olive. As soon as it touched the bottom, with nothing but the olive on the hook, they felt a strong tug on the end of the line. Lilly got very excited and they pulled the line up together very slowly so whatever they caught would not get away. When Lilly saw that it was a huge flounder she was so thrilled and realized that they had prayed the command in the name of Jesus and immediately a fish bit the line. Unbelievable Lilly thought that even the fish obeyed His name. Her son within a minute after that caught a blue fish with the pole. Then David threw the line with the pole back in the water with another olive on it and caught an eel. Nobody on the dock was getting anything. People were looking at Lilly and the family and wondering why they were catching anything when it seemed like not too many fish were biting at that time. They stayed for a while and did not catch anything else and the Spirit said to David, "I gave you your dinner in the first five minutes, the rest of the time you didn't need to stay for." The sense of humor of God! Lilly laughed when he told her what he felt the Lord had said to him. It made sense and they went home and ate fish for dinner that night. If God tells us he gives us each day our daily bread, then I guess He means what he says! God took care of them.

The children were invited to go swimming in a friend's pool but it got canceled and they were so upset that they were crying. It was so very hot and they just were so disappointed. Lilly told them to go and pray and ask God if we could get a pool. They did pray for a pool and a fellow Christian brother showed up with a pool he had just bought for the kids. He said that on his way down the road the Lord told him to go and buy the pool for the children. He listened and the Lord answered the children. A pool. Wow again! God does these things when you walk with Him. Lilly's son prayed to be able to get some baseball bats and he specifically prayed for a metal bat. Wouldn't you know the same man who bought the pool happened to be at another church and they were getting rid of their baseball equipment for some new things so he took them for David and Lilly's church? There was one metal bat just what Lilly's son had asked for. Coincidence? No! He is faithful to forgive us too when we fall on our face.

During this same time, there was a family who came into the church who had a son in law who let's say was not what he made himself out to be. The first day when Lilly met him the Spirit of God told her to watch out for him. Lilly was also discerning human spirits and would just know things about people that were necessary to know. He had more than one spirit he was listening to. At that time, they had moved into this family's house and were living in their basement. This man was no longer himself but a combination of his person and the demons who now have morphed into him. When I say morphing it means they are more than just hanging around from the outside they get closer and closer to us as we allow them to through sin. They will get into your mind too if you keep walking in the life of sin and rebellion.

The next thing you are being controlled by them and you think it is you when in fact it is them. They do not come unless we somehow, someway allow them too. Lack of knowledge is usually the main reason and also sin. One night these beings influenced him enough to where he was going to come and shoot David and Lilly because he was sick of Godly people living in his house. The demons were ticked off about it because they no longer had control and they had to be eliminated. Lilly and her husband knew this in The Spirit and prayed against it and nothing happened. He tried several times to create problems for them including having a few men break the front window to their van. He acted like he was this great Christian and yet he was the opposite. Wolves in sheep's clothing they call them. This man ended up having a massive heart attack and was in the hospital in bad shape. Lilly and her husband went to pray for him even though he did all these things. He got miraculously healed. Figure that one out. God was showing him the love that Christians really had by forgiving and helping a soul in need.

Lilly woke up one day and knew it was time to move out of the basement and into their own place. She just knew. They found a home where her children were going to school and it was a nice home with a built-in pool in the backyard. The kids loved it and Lilly was thankful God made the way for them to be free from this family. They had real issues and there were plenty of demons to go around. Lilly was learning from experience that Christians had these evil spirits hanging around them more than they realized. This family had two that were quite obvious. They were very loving people but the son tried to molest Lilly's son one day. That was a shocker to all but her son's angel motivated him to walk out of the room and tell David. It was time to go for sure and Lilly got the knowing that God was going to make the way. God did make the way. He always did.

God did an amazing thing in this new house with the pool that really put Lilly over the top in her trust with the Lord. They were behind on paying their bills and Lilly was so tired of it. She really did not understand why there was always this struggle with money. She cried all day long in frustration and begged God to please help her get the money she needed to get caught up. She was so emotionally upset and her tears were true. She was really calling out to her Father God to help her in the dilemma she was in. That night they had a prayer meeting and a woman came in and went over to David and asked him how much money he needed. He was surprised at the question because nobody even knew they were behind. He told her he did not even know how much they actually needed. She said, "that was the answer I was looking for because I was going to give you $3,000 dollars but the Lord told me if you said you did not know the amount I was supposed to give you $5,000 dollars." She wrote a check out for $5,000 and Lilly wanted to fall to her knees right there when she found out what she did. Lilly's faith took a leap ahead and she would never forget what God had done for her.

They had a center where they had housing for those in need and one day two men came in looking for a place to stay. They sat down and Lilly could see the spirit influencing the one man. We all know from this story that Lilly is a bit shy so what she said next had to be the move of The Holy Spirit. She looked at the one man and said the Lord has shown me that you are trouble and you will not be able to stay in our house. He looked offended but just as she said those words, the police came in and arrested him. These gifts are valuable for the working of the church and Lilly was definitely called. These gifts were just normal for Lilly as she sensed many things about people from a young age. Lilly was not a perfect person and she had her share of doing things she should not have done but the Spirit was perfecting her and she was becoming more and more spiritual as time went on.

Lilly missed her period and bought the pregnancy test to see what was going on. This was so exciting because God had told her she was going to have a baby boy so this might just be it. The test showed positive and Lilly was so excited. Fourteen days had gone by and everyone was told. They were all accepting this great news when all of a sudden Lilly started to bleed. She did not feel like anything was wrong but it was as if she had gotten her period. Lilly was freaking out right now and feeling very discouraged and angry at God. "Is this some kind of a joke," she yelled in her frustration to the Lord? She went to have a blood test done to see if she had been pregnant and lost the baby but the test showed she was never pregnant, to begin with. The test she took was wrong and showed a false positive. Lilly felt this had to be some kind of a demonic attack to blow her away. It did just that. It took time for Lilly to move on from that, hit and run attempt, of the evil one. Did the devil actually do anything? We will never really know but it sure felt like an emotional assault. Lilly now had some idea of how it felt to have a miscarriage even though she really didn't. It sure felt like it. Where is this promise of a baby that God had told her? She was not getting any younger she thought. "Maybe you are imagining it," said the demon. Maybe no demons were involved in the false test but I know one thing for sure they certainly were involved in the negative feelings everyone felt after the fact. Lilly sensed every one of them as they taunted her into feeling such despair. The anger at God invited in a whole slew of these rat-like creatures who scurried all about the house just jumping from person to person. The demons were loud and clear and Lilly almost believed them but she said, "no, God told me and I saw this baby boy." She moved on battling discouragement!

4. Death and Life Are in His Hands

This chapter we will start with a miracle of God that you may find hard to believe. I assure you this was witnessed by several people who were there and saw it actually happen. Remember that Lilly was told she was going to have this baby boy? She waited about seven years before this word from the Lord would come to pass. She agonized over it while the demon tormented her mind telling her it would never happen. The year when it finally happened, believe it or not, it was the first time I think that David actually acknowledged that the word given to Lilly was real. He had more fear that Lilly was imagining this than that God had spoken to her. This particular day when the timing was right he spoke life into the womb for this child to come into existence. David actually laid his hand on Lilly's stomach and commanded life to be in the name of Jesus. I have to say that it had to be the move of The Holy Spirit. It was most amazing because it was the first time he had done this in the seven years of trying. Guess what happened? You guessed it, Lilly conceived. She had no idea and was so discouraged at this point after waiting and watching all these other women get pregnant after she would pray that she really had almost given up. She gave it to the Lord and told him she was going to stop fighting for things to happen. She surrendered to the will of God whatever it was going to be. The persistent demon that discouraged her for seven years was about to leave because when she realized she was late her daughter told her she looked different. Lilly had let it go so she did not want to hear anything that would get her thinking about it. She answered back that she did not want to hear it but the daughter insisted she go to the doctor to see. While the snow was falling to the ground, Lilly jumped in her car and went to find out from the doctor to make sure some store test would not give her a wrong reading like what had happened before. Slipping and sliding all the way to the doctor in the snow Lilly went at the request of her daughter. The test was quick and Lilly went back home to wait for the results. Mind you, this was some years after the false positive reading and Lilly was just about done with this whole ordeal of these annoying thoughts constantly going in her head of "your just crazy and old."

She was so done, and of course, she wanted to have heard the voice of God in this, but too much torment, and if God had really said it He would make it happen. Lilly still did not have all this knowledge about this spiritual realm and how it functions so closely with us. She knew about demons but to the degree, they interact with people, she had no idea yet. She was learning through each experience in life. Waiting was not one of her favorite things to do and holding onto what she believed was a word from the Lord without any results yet, and had her so wound up it was just constant pressure for her. Was, this time, any different than the others when she believed a lie and got hit right between the eyes with it? She would not allow herself to get excited. It was not going to happen to her again where she was expecting to be pregnant and was not. Lilly went and took the test and came home and went about her business. As a matter of fact, she did not even tell her husband so she would not disappoint him if it was another false alarm! A few hours later the phone rang and I do believe this was one of the most exciting moments of her life. Not because the doctor told her she was pregnant but because she had heard from God. She actually had heard the voice of God and that was the thrill of her life. She was excited about the baby too because God had put this desire in her heart. She picked the phone up and was told the test was positive. Lilly made sure she double checked what they were saying by asking "I am pregnant, right?" The response was yes and then the reaction of Lilly followed as she hung the phone up and ran down the hall screaming out loud, "I am pregnant, I am pregnant!" She scared her husband half to death because she screamed so loud and came running. He did not even know she had gone to the doctor so he had no idea what was happening! Waiting all those years for it to happen finally came to an end and it was no longer faith that made this message from God real but fact. A vision from the one and only true God had just come to pass and Lilly was in heaven in her soul!

Now that we know Lilly is pregnant let me tell you what actually happened when David prayed for Lilly to conceive! That moment when he laid his hand on her stomach a word from God was about to manifest itself. There is so much we miss when our eyes are closed to this spiritual realm. Every time life begins there is an impact of energy that bursts forth as the new life begins.

When the spirit that God gives us is placed into the egg and the connecting of the sperm with that egg creating a new life there is an amazing release of life-giving power that bursts with such force and can be seen in the realm of the spirit. When David placed his hand on Lilly the power of God was released for the egg to be fertilized by the sperm. The sperm became energized and hit the egg which became a living soul. The energy boost from the creation of a life sent out a brilliant light that could be seen by all who were watching from the spiritual side of things. A blast of life was created and a living soul was made with a spirit, a soul and the body that was still in the process of being formed. The God of the universe every time a woman gets pregnant actually does breathe the breath of life into it. The burst of light shows a life being created. There is no physical body yet but never the less, alive. Marcos, Lilly's guardian angel stood by and watched this life being created by the Most High God. We just do not get it down here. The miracles that go on daily we just take for granted because it is part of this world we live in. God intervenes in our lives all the time and we do not even know it. The angels that keep watch over us are busy twenty-four seven. They never sleep and they do battle all the time against evil. Thank God we have these most beautiful spirits that were created by God just like we were. Only we were created in His image and likeness. Think about that for a minute. If that actually sinks into your soul your life will never be the same again! It means we look like Him and should act like Him. That is so amazing and to think that we are more like God than we even know is so fantastic. This is God we are talking about! Wow, and now Lilly is pregnant! God said it and that settled it!

This is great but this is not even the miracle I am talking about when I say how unbelievable some of the things were that God did in Lilly's life. Read on, because you will find some of this hard to believe. By the time Lilly was going to have this baby she was going to be almost forty years old. From the get go, she was considered a high risk just because of her age. That is all normal and the only issue she actually had was she was considered a gestational diabetic which means only during pregnancy your sugar goes up. That too is not so bad and with diet, she kept it under control. Lilly felt great and was so thrilled. The doubting, tormenting imp left the scene because his assignment was now over since there was proof the pregnancy existed. The focus was on the new baby coming and of course, God said it would be a boy. She hoped she had heard the Lord correctly in that part of it. Her husband was fearful of losing the baby but Lilly had no fear what so ever because God had said it and it happened. She had the usual blah feelings in the beginning but was so overwhelmed it did not matter. She rested because she was tired which was normal too. Never underestimate the enemy because his plan for this baby and Lilly was kept secret until the very end and Lilly was caught unaware and so was everyone else. The father had a fear of the baby dying and not sure why and not sure if death should have been rebuked but it hit the fan the day Lilly went to the hospital. Her water broke so she had to go. She was not in labor yet but because the water broke they had to keep her there. For three days Lilly stayed in the hospital waiting for her labor to actually start. It was a bit unsettling as she listened to all the women screaming and crying while they were having their babies, and she was still waiting to go into labor herself. Lilly started to get a bit fearful knowing her suffering was coming soon enough. Finally, the real thing began and it was like a nightmare. The pain was, well we all know, and then she was ready to push the baby out but she was not fully dilated so they told her she could not push yet. That in itself was the hardest thing Lilly had to do and it stressed her out. They finally induced her and although she was going to have natural child birth she took an epidural for the pain. Maybe her age had something to do with her getting so tired and Lilly just wanted this to be over.

When they finally told her she could push the baby out she did just that and with one push she found herself floating somewhere. She was no longer in her body and was looking around trying to figure out where she was. It looked like a file room to her but she had no idea. Then she realized something was not right and she got a bit nervous when she could not remember where she was or what she was doing. She focused her mind on what was happening to her at this moment in time. She saw the number 124 in front of her face and then remembered she was in the middle of having a baby. She got startled when she realized she was pushing out her baby and did not know what had actually

71

happened for those few seconds. At that moment she was back in her body. What was going on in the spirit realm was an all-out battle between good and evil. This is hard to describe but will try my best to explain. It looked like a bunch of elves climbing all over finding mischief to do. One of these beings pulled the spinal tube out of her back that allowed the epidural to work from her spine. The spinal fluid was now leaking out. Another made her leg fall off the side of the bed and another one pulled the wire that was reading the life signs of the baby which was vital. The next demon to show up was death. Yes, you are reading correctly. It was death! It stuck its ugly head into the womb and was messing around with things inside. This creepy thing wrapped the umbilical cord around the baby's neck so it would suffocate and the other had removed the vital sign detector so the plan to kill the prophesied baby was in the works. Lilly had no idea and neither did anyone else. They came in like a bunch of Piranha for the kill. How can they do that when God prophesied this child? This is the unseen danger of the spiritual world around you. Without The Spirit of God revealing this realm we are defenseless against their sneak attacks. Lilly was so involved in the delivery and since God had spoken this baby to her she had no idea this would even happen. A real lesson learned. Never just take anything for granted. Prayer is always needed in all situations and a watchful eye is necessary. Lilly was doing her part in this and finally the midwife told her, "Lilly you have to push right now." There was an urgency in her voice and Lilly was so tired that it was all she could do to push at all. She gave one last push and out came the baby. The baby was taken very quickly and brought over to a table. Lilly was exhausted! There was something going on with Lilly at that point because she was bleeding all over the place. The focus was on the baby though and Lilly felt like she was not even there. Then she heard words that made her heart go right to the floor! "This baby is dead!" She was stunned and asked, "what did I have?" It is a boy the nurse told her. Faith rose up in Lilly because here is the boy the Lord told her she was going to have! The words, "This baby's dead!" were spoken again and her husband repeated them by saying, "My baby's dead?" Lilly looked at him who was standing right in front of her and got righteous anger at him for saying such a thing. The Holy Spirit welled up

72

inside of her because none of it computed. The prophecy from God, the personality told of the child, so death just could not be. Lilly turned towards the lifeless child to the left of her and pointed her finger and spoke these words with power, dominion and authority, "my baby is not going to die in the name of Jesus!" The nurses turned their heads as if she were nuts but when the word JESUS was said, the baby took a breath! Everyone in that room watched the lifeless child begin to breathe. The words were spoken, "my baby is not going to die in the name of JESUS," you have to realize the baby was not just dying he was already pronounced dead. Not just once but twice before Lilly was motivated by the Holy Spirit to say what she said. The Spirit of God spoke as if death did not even happen in His eyes. Not going to die and yet already dead. That has a very heavy meaning to it and shows how our GOD already knew this child was alive. It was the body that stopped functioning but the life of the child was being held somewhere else. Once the baby took the breath the doctors grabbed hold of Lilly and said we need to find out why you are bleeding and they put her up on the table. The doctor told her she would feel uncomfortable as they had to search within her womb to see the problem. The problem had been created by one of the Piranha attacking demons that were there just to bring death into the scene that nobody had any clue about. Lilly got moved once again by The Holy Spirit as she told her husband to lay hands on her and pray for the blood to stop in the name of JESUS. They could not even get a pulse reading on Lilly at that moment as it looked like the enemy was in for not just one kill but to make it a double attack. Once again the Lord came to the rescue because the minute the words were spoken for the blood to stop, it did. Lilly too was saved by the God who created her into the emerald-eyed beauty she was.

Now let me tell you what went on in the Kingdom of God during all of this. The guardian angel of the baby stood by and watched each demon perform their ugly task of making sure the baby died. It did not prevent death because God told it to stand by. When the babies spirit left its body the angel grabbed hold of it and kept it secure until the time the words of life were spoken. The angel put the spirit back into the child and it came back to life. This angel was full of the Son shine from our Lord and has been by his side ever since. At age 2 ½ her son actually remembered this angel grabbing him and keeping him from what he called falling to the ground. He recognized this angel while watching a show about angels on television and telling Lilly that he knew that angel. At his age, all the angels would look alike. Lilly's angel Marcos was working very hard that day as he was standing watch over Lilly to protect her life. He prevented death from taking her life. What was it he did? The death angel sent to cause Lilly to bleed out and fade away from this life was scurrying all around the room trying to grab hold of Lilly while she was bleeding. Marcos stopped him from being able to get to Lilly. Angels have certain powers because they cannot die, so when two angels are battling the force behind them is what pushes back the evil force trying to accomplish a task. So what Marcos did each time was to stand in front of the imp and put up his hands with the Almighty God's power and direct the force right at the imp so he would have to back away. He spoke words of rebuke to create pain within the being as words from Almighty burn because it is like a two-edged sword just like the bible tells us. Tell me that is not a story to tell. One of death and life again where God used Lilly to bring the dead back to life and stopping her own possible death. Yes! Lilly, you are the Emerald-eyed chosen vessel of God. The number 124 which Lilly saw when we believe her spirit left her body we think meant, Lilly who was born Jan. (1), Father's birth is Feb. (2) and all were born on the 4th day of the month, therefore, Lilly was being told again that this baby was coming into this world and will live. Her spirit knew the truth the whole time. May I add right here that her husband the father of this child was anointed too but this is the story about Lilly so we are telling the things she experienced and the story of her husband who went home to be with the Lord would be another book to write because he himself witnessed many amazing miracles too. You will see what actually happened in the life of Lilly and how God even had her life mapped out after He took her husband home. Do not stop here because it gets even more intense and so far, you might be saying how can this all be true! I assure you it is and Lilly and the God of this universe bear witness to it!

Lilly enjoyed her son who was named from the bible. He was a blessing to her in many ways. They struggled financially

74

during this time and life was really hard because of it but the child grew in the spirit of truth as Lilly made sure of it. Things got so bad they ended up stuck up on the hill where they lived without a vehicle and food was, let's say, not in abundance. Lilly kept her focus on her purpose, of loving her God-given son and that kept her from freaking out about the trap they were really in. The winter was even worse because the pipes froze and they had to take snow and boil it to use for cooking, etc. It did not seem that many miracles were happening during this time. Lilly just trusted God believing something would change. She remembered the words spoken to her from several pastors of how God was going to use her mightily and she wondered how that was ever going to happen. She also knew that these things were up to God, not her. Marcos did much ministering during this time of famine. Lilly would take her son out to play in the snow and just enjoy being with him. As far as Lilly was concerned the miracle that she witnessed with her son was enough to last her whole life. How many people do you know who have seen someone die and in the name of Jesus come back to life? This is one of the wow miracles and Lilly was truly thankful she was able to have seen God perform this and allow her to have her son.

They did get out of this poverty mess and went to work for an organization where they helped mentally ill teenagers and when I tell you the demonic activity was running around going crazy that is no exaggeration. Lilly, unbeknownst to her at this time, was living in a home where the demons were actively operating daily. These teenagers were so oppressed by these gremlin looking demons that if you were to actually see them you would probably run for your life, the other way. Marcos had to watch as these creeps tormented these girls. One had a demon of suicide and her fantasy was to jump in front of a train and die. The other would take feces and smear it everywhere. One girl would get so frustrated she would bang her head into the wall. They all wanted to cut their bodies out of frustration and anger so knives or anything that could be used as a weapon had to be locked up. When I say cut their bodies I mean they would find anything sharp and actually cut their own skin with it. Lilly would just know things about these girls but she did not realize yet how she knew. It was just natural to her. One child came home from visiting her dad and Lilly knew she had cut herself with something. Lilly confronted her and she pulled up her shirt and had carved her name on her stomach with the words she was dead. They had many spirit beings tormenting them and we think these beings do not bother us. How can it be explained the reason why someone would look to cut themselves? They were so distraught in their personal lives that these demons grabbed hold of them. They would sit and the demons would talk to Lilly. Lilly had no idea at the time how many demons over the years were actually talking to her because she never realized until later on in her life who these beings were. The girl who fantasized about jumping in front of a train talked with Lilly and explained exactly how she planned on doing it. Lilly watched as she felt excitement about climbing out the window and running to the train station and just taking a leap when the train was about to pass by so she would get hit. She would actually look like she felt joy in this and how sick it was. Lilly knew her son did not need to grow up around this so they made moves to find other work. Through circumstances out of their control, they ended up back in the town where they had left. Demonic activity was running rampant trying to throw them into the street but God had things completely under control. They were hired by a company to watch children again but not so much mental children but just behavior issues. They were well trained for the job but the head of the organization created an issue about them having lived on a government subsidy at one point and told them they did not want them to work for them. It was all so the man who was occupying the home that they were supposed to move into, to watch the children, would not have to move out. It was a scam going on and Lilly and her husband at the time were right in the middle of it. They were told to leave and they had nowhere to go. Lilly almost lost it emotionally because it was like a reenactment of what happened before they left. No money, no job. They had just enough money from the vacation pay that was due them to get a house for rent. They took the company to court and got unemployment benefits so they had enough to keep them going for a while. They ended up back where they lived before in the very town where they fell into poverty. Lilly knew from the beginning they were living in this town for some purpose that God had but had no idea what is was yet. Even though Lilly did not know God was using her with these teenagers who were so influenced by evil she did help them by making them realize that God was on their side and He loved them. Lilly truly felt for them but it also made her feel creepy when dealing with them as she sensed the spiritual realm that was functioning all around her. She was being led to a truth about this world we live in. We are sharing this planet with the devil and his demons because we allowed him into the garden when we listened to him rather than God. Now we have to deal with all this torment unless we are aware of it and come back at it with the power of God. Lilly had this power but had no understanding of how to really use it. Time and patience are what was needed.

They were back in the town that the Lord had led them to the first time. When God places you somewhere for His purpose and you leave that is not good. He will send you back if He really needs you there. So church begins and day care begins. The church helped the mentally ill in town so Lilly was seeing demons on a regular basis. One particular Sunday there was a man who came to church. He needed to take his medication after service so Lilly very gently asked him if he could take them in the other room because she did daycare and if a pill fell to the floor one of the children might pick it up and swallow it. She saw the demon manifest himself by contorting the man's face with a look of hatred and rage. Lilly got a strong knowing to step aside because the demon pushed him in anger to barrel towards the door and he would have knocked her over. She stepped to the right and sure enough he shot out the door. She felt bad but was thankful for the heads up and was quite amazed how she knew before it happened exactly what he was going to do. How do the demons actually do what they do? Take a person who is disturbed about something. Say they are angry about what has happened to them. They dwell on it and dwell on it until it consumes their emotions. There are all these demons hanging around the earth with no bodies to push their feelings on, so they are lost and in need of a place to exist and manipulate. Here you are filled with anger and here the demon is filled with anger. It's the perfect match and the sin of unforgiveness has opened your flesh to join with this spiritual being. You have no clue this being even exists but it does and the only way it can satisfy its feelings is to have a human body or an animal to do it in. It comes around a starts to influence you into a deeper feeling of anger. The longer you stay with those destroying feelings the closer it gets to your soul. At the beginning, it starts whispering to you by hanging around you. As you keep listening to what it says it gets closer and closer to your mind. The next it grabs hold of your mind and then you are really focused on this anger and unless you turn away and get delivered from it, you will stay that way forever. You will never even know why you are angry all the time. People can even get possessed but that rarely happens in this country because we have the Holy Spirit and unless you are a satan worshiper your spirit is protected. Our souls receive many negative seeds over the years of listening to lies and deception. Lilly has seen these lies come out of people's souls like black circles when a person learns a truth. The truth then replaces the lie. Demons are actual beings that will leave when told to in the name of Jesus. The circles are like weeds growing in a garden that needs to be plucked out so they don't choke the good plants. So to like our souls. Good seeds need to be planted and negative seeds need to be removed or plucked out. Truth replaces lies.

One day another demon went crazy as Lilly was watching children in her daycare. She received a phone call from those in charge of one of the mothers who had emotional issues. Lilly was told when the mom shows up to pick up her children they were not to go with her. The police were coming to take the mom to the hospital because she wanted to kill herself and the children would be in danger. Lilly knew she was going to deal with this demon when it showed up at the door. She was ready for it to show its ugly head. The mom shows up at the door and Lilly can see in her eyes this demonic force glaring at her. With a smirk, the mom says, "I am here to pick up the kids." Lilly tells her she is not allowed because she was looking to hurt herself and the kids were not safe with her right now. She told her to wait and get the help she needs and the demon proceeded to get nasty. The demon began blurting out obscenities back at Lilly and the mom was insisting on her giving her the children. Lilly felt bad for the mom but had no choice but to wait for the police to come and get her. The mom left and screamed all the way down the street all kinds of nasty things about Lilly being a terrible daycare provider and not caring about the kids, and Lilly was the devil. It was unbelievable and you tell me where does that kind of thing come from if not from a source of pure evil intentions? Lilly witnessed many times these spiritual beings acting out over the years so there was no denying it to her. She watched it from time to time so she knew that these beings did exist and did torment people. How disgusted it made her feel. To take a child of God and just destroy it was terrible but so real.

Do not think that just because you love the Lord you cannot be oppressed by one of these beings. I came back to this point in the book to add this demonic story because the enemy is looking to do what? Stop the work of God in this world so he can take over. The way he does it is to attack the children of God. He does it every way and anyway he can. Physical attacks and emotional attacks are his main weapon and demons do not even care if they stick around when we are in church. Remember they came from a holy place and know all about it. Lilly has actually watched demons manifesting in church acting as if they were part of it all. There are demons who try to act like Jesus and want to be worshiped so they look for their own glory right in the churches. The wolves in sheep's clothing are some but then there are people who love the Lord and have had emotional trauma and spirits have come along and influenced them. They have some real emotional issues but truly love the Lord. Lilly has seen many of them over the years and these are only a few that I am writing about that she has witnessed. She knew a so-called pastor who knew the word and played the organ and preached with the power of The Holy Spirit. He became friends with her and she started noticing that some of the things he was telling her just did not add up. It seemed like he was lying and making up stories. This very much disturbed Lilly because she had grown to love this preacher friend and she did know he had been abused by his mother. She had no idea that a person could be such a great preacher of the word and could be so messed up. She found out over time that he had a drinking problem and he was a chronic liar. He had few other issues that we will not go into and are irrelevant to the story but the point is this man, a preacher of the word, one who loved the Lord, had demons. Lilly was stunned and the way she knew for sure that he had these demons is because he called her one night and had been drinking. The spirits began to speak through him right to Lilly and they screamed and yelled obscenities and Lilly witnessed all of this firsthand. She knew demons were real but she was learning that even those who loved the Lord could have them. That was scary to her. The demons talked out loud through people too. Lilly watched many more demons over the years manifest themselves.

When Lilly was around them they would openly reveal themselves and it was as if they could not control their feelings but would act out in her presence. The reason for this was the anointing. It could be a simple thing like jealousy that the person thinks are their own feelings. They would just act out when she was near them. She walked into a diner one day and passed by someone sitting in a booth and as she walked by with her husband the person started to bark like a dog. Lilly and her husband looked at each other and were shocked. Several times while being in a restaurant she commanded demons across the room to stop acting out and they shut right up. This kind of thing became normal for Lilly. Without a doubt, these beings exist and are functioning on planet earth. How disgusting it was to Lilly to know that these creatures were using children of God to get their kicks from their uncontrollable desire to do whatever they were. They had no regard for humans accept to use them. You can call them many different names. Lust, anger, rebellion, stubbornness, guilt, fear, insecurity, murder, suicide and I am sure I could go on and you get the point. Lilly was feared by these spirits because they knew she recognized them and she was given the name of Jesus to use against them.

Remember just as many of these creepy beings that are around, there are more angelic beings, who influence and come into the scene to save us from harm. There are angels that inspire us when we need it. I will explain much more clearly about these angelic beings when we get further into the story about Lilly. Her life with this spiritual realm was just beginning still and she actually steps into a more powerful spiritual realm as time goes on in her life.

This next story will once again blow your mind. As you can see Lilly was watching evil all the time but her personal life was filled with love and joy in knowing God was with her and her family. Her son, the miracle baby, was in school and was growing

80

and learning. She was a minister and knew her life was to help those in need. Each time she dealt with evil she knew that God had the ultimate say in all of it. There was definitely conflict in this life and the only answer to Lilly was God. One of the members of the church had some emotional issues and on this particular day, she was getting attacked by a spirit who wanted to take her life. She has no idea what was spiritually going on at this time and just went along with her feelings. Feelings can kill us if we listen to them rather than God. She was so wrapped up in the negatives of her life she decided to take her life. The demons were talking to her all day trying to convince her that her life was not worth living. They relentlessly kept repeating over and over again that the only way out for her was to take her life. Even though she knew that suicide was wrong they repeated it so many times that they convinced her it was the thing she needed to do. How did they do it? There was one on one side speaking in her ear and there was another one on the other side saying the same thing. It was enough to drive anyone crazy. It did just that because she did something that she knew was against her God. After she swallowed a bottle of pills she got moved to call Lilly who was her pastor. She told Lilly what she did and Lilly called 911 and drove around the corner to her house. She ran up the stairs and told her to go and make herself throw up the pills. It did not work because she had taken the pills too long ago. At that moment she slumped to the ground and Lilly yelled out, "satan you will not kill her in the name of Jesus." At that moment the ambulance came and they took her to the hospital and she was in a coma. The doctors said she took enough pills to kill more than one elephant. She should have died but death was stopped through the powerful prayers of The Holy Spirit and Lilly who was able to follow His leading. She was chosen to save lives and since her childhood, it was in her soul to do so. After becoming an adult and learning many truths she was able to allow the moving of the Spirit of God to do these great miracles. Lilly in all humility just took it in stride and never once thought who she was even when her prayers brought people back to life from the dead already and stopped death right in its tracks when the words were spoken. Lilly was a true child of God with all the gifts operating in her life. Call her an apostle or prophet she was too humble to ever use a title. All she desired to do was serve the Lord and do whatever He wanted her to do.

One more amazing miracle to share and this one was a real battle. Lilly and her husband bred dogs to bring in funding to the ministry and a man came one day to buy a dog from them. He told them both that he did not want to come in when he saw the ministry sign in front of the house about the Lord. He was Jewish. He came in anyway because he traveled a bit to get there. He picked out his dog and told them it was for his daughter who had cancer and was very ill. Lilly and her husband told him they would go and pray for her if he wanted them too. He said thank you and left. A few weeks went by and he called and said his daughter was very ill and he wanted to know if they would come and pray for her. They told him they would but this was a five-hour trip just to get there so it was a day of traveling. It was not what Lilly really wanted to do but she knew he was Jewish and it would be a great witness to him that Jesus is the Messiah. He was also told that if they came they would be praying in the name of Jesus. He said he understood that and his daughter was very ill and it did not matter to him how they prayed. He knew their ministry sign said they believed in miracles and that was what she needed. The morning when Lilly and her husband were ready to go her husband fell to the floor with such back pain he could barely walk. He came over to her and told Lilly and she looked at him and he looked at her and they both knew they had to go anyway. A life was in need and they would have to put themselves to the side. Her husband told her he could not drive and Lilly freaked out a bit. She hated to drive any distance and now a ten-hour trip without a clue where this place was. Panic set in a bit but she focused on the Lord and knew she would have to deal with it just like her husband had to deal with the pain. They were on their way. Both were very uncomfortable. Lilly was then told by her husband that he would need to be brought up in a wheelchair. Lilly looked at him and said, "are you kidding me? We are going to pray for this girl and we are coming up in a wheelchair? That is going to look insane. Physician heal thyself." Lilly was so disturbed about all this and was embarrassed on top of it all. She was going to have to wheel him in. "Are you sure God, we are supposed to be doing this?" she blurted out loud. After taking five hours to get there they pulled into the hospital parking lot and right by the door was a wheelchair as if it was waiting for them. Her husband, in severe pain, hobbled over to the wheelchair and sat down. Lilly wheeled him up and there she was in a room of isolation. Bald and pale as a ghost. They had to put on masks and special booties to cover their shoes. They had to get sterile so they would not bring in any germs because her white blood cell count was so low that she could die from any germs. They both walked in the room after explaining the wheelchair and laid hands on her and prayed for healing in the name of Jesus. Immediately color came back to her face and everyone noticed it. Lilly's husband leaned over and whispered in her ear to get him out of there he was about to get sick from the pain. The mom on their way out said, "can you see the color back in her face?" They said, "yes!" and left. The ride home was the real nightmare of the day because her husband was getting sick in the back seat from pain. Lilly missed the turn off to get home so she had to go the long way around. It was now dark and she was so upset about her husband that she yelled out to God, "please heal this girl. We are both suffering God and at least let her get healed." Then they passed by a sign that had the girls name in large letters on it. That was amazing! Lilly was taking her husband right to the emergency room when they got home. They finally pulled into their village and her husband said to her, "you're not going to believe this, but I have no more pain." Lilly looked at him and realized it was an attack to stop them and they went anyway so God delivered her husband on the spot when they got home. It was all a test. What an unbelievable story and the lengths the devil will go through to stop the children of God from doing things. The phone call came through the next day that the girl's white blood cell count was normal and the doctors were going nuts trying to figure out what had happened. They were all Jewish and Jesus had healed the daughter. She was out of the hospital within the week and glory to God she went mountain climbing with the family after that. They sent Lilly and her husband a picture of the family, all were well and she had hair on her head. Lilly still has this picture today. Who is this emerald-eyed beauty? Is she still alive? What else has the Lord done with her? Just want to say here that the gifts of The Spirit are for all the children of God but most never use them and never know they even exist. Lilly is one who has been chosen to shine the Glory of the Lord!

5. Touch Not Mine Anointed

I have to put my observation out at this point because over the years I have seen some unbelievable things happen when people have come against Lilly on a personal level. You can come up with your own conclusion but I have already come up with mine. To me, there can be no other explanation for some of these situations that happened except for the sheer fact that God gave retribution for what these people did to Lilly. The first story and this happened when her children were young and in school. They were living in a town and they had to move away because of financial reasons. The children were halfway through the school year and somehow the school district found out they had moved out of the school district. Instead of allowing the children to finish out the year they threw the kids out of the school. Lilly begged them to please give them a chance to move back into the area and not to break the children's hearts by just throwing them out. There was absolutely no compassion for the children who were involved in school activities, friendships, etc. Lilly's daughter was involved in a play and absolutely loved her teacher. When I tell you that Lilly begged, it was heart-wrenching how she pleaded with them to just give them time to move back into the distinct so the children would not be heart broken. Nobody cared and Lilly watched her children cry and she felt responsible because money was tight and they had to suffer because of it. Her daughter went into class to have the teacher sign her year book early because she was leaving and what happened next is just scary. That day was the last day her daughter would see this teacher who she loved so much and that very same day after school ended the teacher went into the hospital and never came out because she died. I don't know about you but that is just a little bit too bizarre for me. Explanation? None, except God, intervened and decided nobody else was going to have her for their teacher either. Nobody knew who told the office that Lilly had moved out of the district either. Coincidence, I think not! The bible tells us not to touch God's anointed and to do His prophets no harm. One of the prophets in the bible was called names by a few children in the village. They thought it was funny that he was bald and proceeded to call him

85

baldy, baldy. The next thing that happened was they got killed by a wild animal. God takes it very serious when anyone comes against His chosen prophets. Who is this Lilly? Lilly herself was in shock when she found out that none of the other children were going to see this woman again either and she wondered at the timing of the teacher who was young to just up and die. This is not the only time that something like this happened.

The family was living in this house before they had to move and there was a farm behind them that had strawberries growing. It was a whole field full of strawberries so some of the neighborhood boys snuck in to pick them. They ran through the backyard of the house where Lilly lived after the owner tried to catch them. He did catch them and began to throw the boys all over the place. Lilly ran to the back door and yelled at the man to stop hurting the boys. The man began to scream at Lilly blaming her for the boys trying to escape through her yard. Lilly told him to tell their parents and that he had no right to beat them up physically. He cursed and yelled at her and then the man's father pulled into Lilly's driveway with the cops. Lilly's husband came running from the back room and told the guy to stop screaming at Lilly. It was an ordeal. Angry demons were acting out all over the place. The children were wrong but this violent spirit was flinging these boys around like they were rag dolls. Lilly could not stand by and just watch it happen. Lilly watched as the man was almost out of control with rage. There was a demon hanging on his back just screaming obscenities and the words that were being spoken by this neighborhood farmer were being manipulated by this enraged spirit. In other words, what the demon was actually saying was being spoken by this man. That is amazing and pretty creepy at the same time. It was word for word what this thing was saying and nobody knew that it had taken over the man's emotions except the angels of God and of course the demons. This demon was releasing its own rage through this man who obviously had allowed this spirit into his life. The spirit was ripping his back with its claws as the man was swinging his arms all over the place as the children were being flung to the ground. He would grab one child and throw him and then grab another child and throw him too. The demon was in such a frenzy of rage that the man had no idea this supernatural imp was actually controlling his behavior. It was creepy. Lilly was not completely aware of this realm yet but she did sense that this behavior was a bit over the top for a few boys who were shoving some strawberries in their mouths. Here come the police. Lilly had to explain what was going on and nobody got in trouble. The father of the man just stood quiet but he was the instigator who brought the police into the picture. There was no need for the police because Lilly had not done anything wrong except tell the man to stop hurting the children. It was his son who had started the whole issue. It really upset Lilly because she was a peaceful person but just could not stand by and watch this man touching these young boys. Everybody finally left and the father who called the police had a massive heart attack and died that night. Another unsolved mystery! Hey, Emerald-eyed beauty, remind me never to mess with you and your God. This was not the only time things happened when people came against Lilly.

There was a time when Lilly and her husband were involved in helping a bakery out and were given the leftover buns to give to the needy. Business exploded when Lilly and her husband came on board. The owners got greedy as the cash was coming in very quickly and they did not want to share any of the money with them. The wife of the owner went to see a fortune teller who told her what she needed to do was to ask Lilly and her husband to leave so they would not have to share any of the profits that were coming in. Lilly told her she was not listening to God but was listening to the advice of the devil. The woman so full of greed ignored what Lilly said, Lilly and her husband were asked to leave. All for the sake of greed. They left but before walking out the door Lilly warned her that God was not happy with their decision. What they had not realized was the business prospering was only because God had blessed it because of Lilly and her husband. Take away God and take away His blessings. The business had been open for years but one week later the doors were shut because they had no business anymore. This was a business that was making a lot of money obviously because the favor of God was on it while Lilly and her husband were there. I guess we need to really learn from these situations that Lilly is experiencing. Once again the word does say touch not mine anointed and do my prophets no harm. It sure seems like it's true when you see these things happen.

A large furniture store shut down too after they refused to give back a deposit, that the church was owed and never did return it. All of these situations happened on their own without anyone rebuking or saying a word against them. God is the judge.

They met a pastor who came into one of their food outreach centers at the time and he seemed nice enough. They got to know him and they even were invited to dinner a few times and had a good time in the Lord. Lilly and David were going to the different motels where the needy were living who were homeless and bringing them meals. This pastor got jealous when one of the local news channels found out and came to do a story about how they were feeding the people. Lilly ended up on the news and this man got so upset that he called Lilly and asked her why she was on the news. Lilly told him they just wanted to do a story about it and he said, "how come they did not do a story about me? He then proceeded to tell her he was going to call the news station and tell them they were fakes." Lilly openly rebuked what he said and told him, "you better get on your knees and repent from that jealous spirit and the lies you have been spreading about us." He was going places and telling them that Lilly and her ministry was not legitimate. This was a man who was supposed to be their friend. Lilly was in shock about this whole thing. She could not understand what had made him act this way. That was the end of any relationship they had and a few days later Lilly received a phone call that the man had gone crazy and they had to put him away because of it. Lilly was again stunned and knew that because of what he did by lying about her and the ministry work she was doing he lost his mind. Lilly felt very sad but once again she knew how dangerous it was to touch God's anointed. She had seen it before and here it had happened once again. Lilly in her humility still never looked at herself as one of God's anointed. She just knew she loved the Lord! Obviously, God saw different in who she was.

When Lilly was young there was a teacher who walked with her to school and made her feel extremely uncomfortable. He made sure he was right there to walk with her every day and every day he would ask her all kinds of questions about her life.

Lilly was very shy and hated what felt like an invasion of her privacy. He thought she was the cutest thing and would tell her all the time how pretty she was. It made Lilly so nervous and he seemed like a nice guy but her feeling uncomfortable was very real. She tried to walk fast so he would not see her but without fail there he was waiting to walk with her. Lilly would die each time he showed up. She did not even know how he was able to be there at the same time as her. He must have lived near the school and walked to school like Lilly did every day. Lilly hated it and just was not comfortable because he made her out to be some really special child. He knew all about her good grades and he would tell her I cannot wait to have you in my sixth-grade class. Lilly knew he expected her to be this perfect little child so she just did not want to get him and have to deal with the attention. She did not know why she felt so nervous around him but she was so concerned about getting him as her sixth-grade teacher. She just did not like him even though he was extremely nice to her. Who knows what Lilly sensed but what Lilly did know was she did not want him as her teacher. The year when Lilly was going into sixth grade, this teacher, left the school district after teaching there for many years. Lilly was in awe at his leaving and wondered if God had made him move away or it is possible he might have died. Never did find that out. What was it that made her feel so uncomfortable about him? There were times when Lilly did not even know herself. They were just feelings of knowing something was not right. She developed this gift as she got older and was more matured in her life and in her knowledge of the word of God. There is still so much more to tell and some truly remarkable stories to share about this green-eyed woman of God. Keep on reading because this green-eyed beauty lived with the hand of God by her side and many times He stepped in to save her. What a great God we have and Lilly can attest to it!

Lilly was living in a place called Long Island, New York. She had lived on Long Island her entire life in a town called Lindenhurst. They were feeding the needy everywhere and they had rented a storefront building to open a pantry to feed the needy from. They used this place to generate funds by having lunches made and some soda's and coffee and candy and they had breakfast every morning and all the proceeds went to helping feed the needy. They were giving away food for free from this place too and the devil saw fit to harass them once again. He called a meeting of the demons and ordered several of them to influence some people to break into the store and steal from them. The store was about a half hour drive from where they were living and on this one particular day when they arrived they noticed the window had been broken and some things were ransacked. They had left a bunch of quarters in the cash register and left the draw open so if anyone did come to steal they would at least not break the register. All the money was gone and some of the food. They reported it to the police and Lilly was upset because they were giving this food away for free and why would anybody have to steal it. The very next day a man walked in, while Lilly was alone in the store and opened up his hand to show her all the quarters he had to buy a piece of candy. He looked directly into Lilly's eyes and smirked as he picked up a candy bar and handed Lilly the amount due in quarters. Lilly looked back at the man and said, "you have a lot of quarters I see." The man smirked again and said, "yes I do." Lilly could see the demon and knew it was the very person who has robbed them the night before. She kept her mouth shut because there was no proof and she was also alone in the store. She was angry about it because she just knew he purposely came in to brag and to throw it in her face that he had stolen from them and got away with it. Lilly wished she could just rebuke him to his face but when dealing with demons you have to have the wisdom of God and if a person wants to live in that sin the demon will tell you. "take a walk this person wants me here." Six times the store was robbed and once it was robbed on David's birthday. Lilly cried and felt so bad. The police put a silent alarm in to catch the burglar and they had to just wait until he would make his moves again. Her husband David had a vision of a man coming in with a gun and pointing it at Lilly. The decision is made to move away from Long Island and find a place of peace where the vision of the community could be built. At this time all that was known about the community was that Christians would live there. Nobody knew it was going to be during the tribulation yet. The person gets caught but there were two who had actually stolen from the store. David and Lilly moved before they ever could see who the one person was. The other person was a man who came in for free food all the time and was very friendly to them. It really upset Lilly that a person they helped would do that. Lilly knew the other man was the guy who walked in with all the quarters. The devil robbed them but God used it to push them into moving to the place where the community was meant to be built. God does use all things to accomplish His purpose.

They did move upstate and struggled with finances and moved so many times that Lilly stopped counting. She was so stressed about it all the time but continued to trust the Lord. God always made a way for them. Maybe not in the traditional way all the times but He never let them go hungry. A local store threw out a bunch of frozen food one day because their refrigeration had broken down. David went looking each day for scraps to feed the pigs they had so he discovered all this food that was sitting in boxes by the dumpsters. It was the perfect time because there was nothing left to eat in the house. Lilly cried when he brought home the food. There was even a piece of cake. Who would think that you could find perfectly good food thrown away but that day a broken freezer fed Lilly and her family for a week. A few times David found lobsters with the tails removed but the entire rest of the lobster was intact and was still cold. It must have been thrown out just before he showed up. Who do you know throws away lobsters? They just wanted the tails to sell but Lilly enjoyed making a lobster sauce with them. This may seem hard to believe but another day when David went looking for food to feed the pigs he found steaks, two complete filet mignon, that were placed in a box by the dumpster. They were perfect and that was a real blessing for them. David thought that maybe someone in the store was trying to steal them and put them in the back to take home and he just happened to come while they were sitting by the garbage. To this day nobody knows how they got there but they were very thankful for it. As you can see God was feeding them. If the Lord chooses to send food from a raven do not complain about it. He did it in The Word. Lilly feeds the birds and the ravens all the time and she always says to herself, "if times get hard the ravens will bring food for sure." She truly believes it. Are these miracles? Maybe, they were put there by the hand of God! What matters is that God provides for those He loves!

This part of her life was quite devastating but God had a purpose in it. At the time Lilly did not know but we do not always know what God is doing and why He is doing it. This may be another coincidence to you but in my book, I think not. Lilly walked through town one day asking all the local businesses to help them in their feeding the needy with the soup kitchen they had. She felt humiliated asking but she did it anyway believing it was what God had asked her to do. She got only a few responses and felt terrible that nobody really cared for the hurting families. It was what it was and Lilly moved on and continuously helped those in need. Right after she did this the town got hit with a flood that destroyed the entire town. I will tell you how it all went down or rather up as the floods rose that day. Lilly woke up and noticed that it was raining quite heavily. Her son came back from walking to the river that ran a few houses down from her. He said, "mom the river is up really high. "Lilly got a knowing right then that something was going to happen and she ran out the door to take a look for herself. Her soul jumped with fear and as she headed back to her house. She told her next door neighbor who was a member of her church, that this was going to be bad. Her neighbor looked stunned because Lilly was a very positive person and here she was telling of this gloom to come. Lilly spoke again and told her I am serious get ready because this is going to be bad. Lilly moved as quickly as she could and let all the dogs out and back in immediately after they did their thing. She took extra food and through it in their crates. She looked at four puppies that were in a bottom crate and she had a thought that she better pick them up and put them into one of the higher crates. She had no idea what was about to happen but she knew it was going to be bad. Within those few minutes of running around trying to get things organized Lilly looked out back and saw the water rushing into their yard. Fear hit Lilly and her husband David said, " we are out of here." He said, " Lilly if we don't leave now we will be stuck in this house." Lilly was so upset because she had seventeen champion blood line poodles in crates and here was the river rushing into their back yard. The one poodle they had who was the one who started all the breeding was grabbed by their son as he said, "we are taking Princess with us." There was no argument from Lilly but she was heartbroken having to leave the others with whatever fate was going to happen. Lilly was so emotional that tears were streaming down her face as the three of them and the dog ran to the car with the water rushing all around them. They had to drive over the bridge where the water was overflowing to get to safety. David just stepped on the gas and they went up the hill to Lilly's daughter's house. She felt terrible having to just show up at her house but they really didn't have much of a choice. Were demons involved in this? I have no idea but all I do know is the river was flooding the town and Lilly and her family were in a safe place. David and his son in law were never on the greatest of terms so this was quite an uncomfortable situation to be in. It was one of those times when everybody just teams up because of tragedy and although Lilly felt a bit uncomfortable the whole flood situation had everyone freaked out. Lilly at this time had no thought of what Noah must have gone through when his family entered the Ark and God shut the door behind them. They knew all the people were going to die except them and it must have been very devastating to them. Lilly cried her eyes out that night thinking of all the dogs she loved and what might be happening to them. She had no idea whether they would drown or be safe. They went back down the road to see how bad things were and the river was raging through the entire town that looked like it was part of the river itself. Lilly's house was surrounded by a rushing river that was out of control and her dogs were trapped there. That night while Lilly laid on the floor she prayed to God and gave Him the whole thing. She could not even cope with thinking about the poor dogs and their fate in all this. She cried and told herself that there was nothing she could do about the animals that had to be left behind. The thunder rumbled in the background as the lightening flashed across the sky. The rain was coming down in torrents and Lilly prayed that they were safe where they were. She could hear the water running down the hill all around the house. It was very frightening just listening to how hard it was raining and all the people who were dealing with this flood. Lilly had never gone through anything like this before and realized the house she always wanted to have by a river was out of the question now. She would never ever live in a house near a river again. She was going to have a place where it would be safe from flooding. Fear was attacking her and I am sure there were a few demons on the loose but Lilly just focused on the will of her God in all this and found peace in the midst of this storm. She even accepted that all the dogs might be found dead and had come to the conclusion that life has its ups and downs and we just have to know that we are loved by our God. We might not like many things we have to deal with but there is always a reason for it all. The next day David, Lilly and their son tried to walk through the water to get back to the house. They all locked arms and began to walk through the rushing water but the force of the river was still way too strong and David said, "we are not going to drown to try and save these dogs." Lilly got upset because she knew the dogs would run out of food and water if they were even alive. It was so disturbing but they had to wait for another day before the water receded enough to get back to the house. The entire town was stuck wherever they were when the river flash flooded the town and nobody was moving until mother nature was willing to release them. There was another day of battle with the emotions of fear and worry about the dogs. Lilly was in the zone of survival and we are all in this together. She consoled anybody that would talk to her. Lilly has that gift of uplifting souls even when she may be down. It was just who she was. She was filled with the glory of God no matter what she was personally going through in her own life. She had the gift of faith and it would always touch others. The day finally comes when they are able to walk through the water that had receded enough and get back to the house. Lilly felt anxious because of what they might find. When they got in front of the house she was stunned at the damage the force of the water had done. The garage had been moved up about six feet with all the stuff in it. The front door was off the hinge and hanging. The back porch was destroyed and ready to collapse. She took a deep breath and went in the front door. The floor was covered with mud and from across the room, flying off the couch, comes one of her dogs who leaped into her arms. Lilly smiled as he covered her with mud. His crate was the only one that had a bungee cord holding it closed so he had escaped. He made it through the flood and must have been swimming in it because they could see the water had been a few feet high in the house itself. The basement was filled completely up and two feet of water was in the house. It had receded by now but the entire house was destroyed. All the

94

furniture was ruined. The floors were bowed up and the doors were off the hinges. What a mess. Lilly was more concerned about the rest of the dogs. She walked in their room where all the dog crates were expecting to find some dogs that did not make it. Lilly was so thankful when she saw all the dogs sitting in their crates. They were covered with mud but were all alive. The water had reached as high as their necks and you could see they had trying to get out because there were scratch marks of mud all over the top of the crates where they had been desperately trying to escape. If Lilly had known how bad this really was going to be she would have let them free upstairs but she had no idea and the flash flood was so quick that there was no time to prepare. With no running water and no house that was really left to live in any more Lilly opened the crates and brought the dogs upstairs. She took what was left of the food that had not gotten wet and just put them in a room until she could figure out what to do with them all. She felt terrible but she had to give them food and water and just leave them for now. The puppies were high enough so they never even got wet. If the water would have been any higher all the dogs would have drowned. Lilly was so thankful to God for saving the animals. Now the problem was what to do with them. She had no house anymore to live in. The Red Cross arrived and they provided money to find housing for the people. Lilly and the family was fed daily at the school by the Red Cross and F.E.M.A. while they cleaned out what they could salvage from the house. Lilly found somebody to take the dogs for her. It was a time of reflecting and just trusting God to show them what was next. The owner had refused to sign the house over after promising for eight years that she would and it got destroyed along with the rest of the town. Lilly had no idea why any of this happened at that time but years later The Holy Spirit opened her eyes. There was a real reason for all of it. Lilly had to move to the place where the vision was meant to happen. This house was not meant for Lilly to buy as it was in the flood zone and could not be a safe haven. Lilly was beginning to learn that God really did have a purpose for everything we go through even when it seems upsetting. To this day the house is still vacant and that happened in 2006. The destruction of that house led Lilly to her house on the hill where it is safe from any floods. The flood represented Noah and the

Ark and the land they live on now and the property behind the house is supposed to be available to help feed the needy during the end time tribulation period. A miraculous message found in the water some thirty years ago is coming to pass. The flood happened and pushed them into this house where the tribulation will happen and as in the days of Noah so to shall it be with the coming of the Son of Man! Flood with Noah, flood with Lilly! Symbolic because God is not going to flood the whole earth again. He will destroy it by fire this time. So this is what is being said: Arks are being built for safety during the end time tribulation period. Lilly has been chosen to be part of building one of these places. She has been being led to this final episode in her life where she will help those in need during the hardest time in the history of the world. The preparation for this has been going on for her whole life. The building of what is called the end time Arks. Will explain more later but let us get back to her life because the power of Almighty God just pours out of her in some of these next true stories. To end this part, I have to just add that Lilly ended up having to give all her dogs to animal rescue because the woman who took them decided she did not want to watch them anymore and to make this short the dogs ended up three hours away from Lilly where the man was not taking care of them. Lilly took this woman at her word that this man was trustworthy but he was not. Demons were really involved in this part of the story because they were stealing from her the money that they were getting from the sale of the puppies. The man was using her dogs to breed to his dogs and did not even tell her. It was a real time of deception and lies and stealing. Lilly rebuked them for what they were doing. Lilly received a phone call from the A.S.P.C.A. telling her the dogs were being mistreated. She cried once again and she knew she had to do something to save these animals once more. She had to let them all go. Help came from the animal rescue people and Lilly showed up with them. Lilly never told the people who had her dogs that she was coming because she thought they would hide her dogs. Lilly and the animal rescue people showed up and the dogs were brought out in these small crates where they could not even move. Lilly's beautiful silver champion blood line male dog was so black she did not even recognize him. It was disgusting and Lilly cried at having to lose her dogs and for the abuse they had to endure. Lilly was hoping to be able to find a place so she could get them all back but it just did not happen. They all ended up in good homes but Lilly lost them all except for Princess who she took with her to the apartment they lived in before they actually got the house. So sad and it broke her heart. It was a chapter in her life she would never want to go through again and learned a real lesson about trusting people. We have to have discernment and we must listen to it. Lilly really did not have a choice because she had no place for the dogs to go and did not want to turn them over to animal rescue. She wanted her dogs back. She loved them all and knew they missed her. Animal rescue was the only salvation at this time.

Lilly would go and pray in the back yard every day just before dusk. This was her favorite time of the day. Things began to wind down and so did her soul. Lilly was such a go getter in life that she pushed herself all the time. She had dealt with some physical issues over the years like kidney stones that repeatedly caused her to have to be operated on. She had a few miraculous healings where the stones were blasted out by God and she did not have to go to the hospital. She also had to go to the hospital and have the doctors do the healing task. On one occasion after having an operation Lilly woke up and was shaking from the anesthesia and lifted her hands up to God for Him to help her stop shaking. As the nurse and the doctor watched she felt a surge come right from the throne of God and hit her body and the shaking stopped immediately. She heard one of the nurses say, "look she is praying." Another time she woke up and had been talking to Jesus in her sleep and when she awoke she was looking for a picture of the Lord and then realized it was not a picture she saw it was Jesus himself speaking to her by a tree in her dream. She did not remember what He said until years later when she finally remembered He was telling her she was healed. There was another time she got prayed over in the church and the power of God hit her so hard that it felt like a truck had run her over. It was so unbelievable to her and she thought if that were not The Holy Spirit I would have broken bones. She got slammed to the ground and the stones were gone and there are x-rays to prove it. That is one time Lilly will never forget. The power was so awesome there was no denying it was the real thing. The force that came out of nowhere while she had people praying over her was so strong that she truly knew God had some real power that He used through His people. A life changing moment for Lilly as she was the one who felt it and saw the results.

I almost forgot to put this in the story but the Lord has been showing me for the past three mornings different situations that happened to Lilly that I had to go back and put in before the final editing is done. This is a really amazing part too in the life of Lilly. It happened in the church like many other supernatural things. I say supernatural only because they are not of this natural world and you will see what I mean as I tell you. Lilly, her future husband, the musician, and a few other members of the church were all standing around Lilly's husband David, before he went home to be with the Lord, and were praying for his back. He was in a lot of pain all the time so they all felt led to pray for him. Lilly had no idea at this time that he was going to die and she was going to end up marrying the musician but what happened next was a life changing experience for Lilly and the others who were there. The pastor stood up after the prayer and raised his hand up towards each person in that room and said the words, "Apostles, Apostles," as he was pointing at each person. Lilly went flying off her feet to the right of her and literally traveled a few feet in the air to the ground. The musician went flying and so did all the others. Lilly was stunned once again in her life at this power of The Holy Spirit. Even though she flew a few feet and ended up on the floor she never felt a thing accept the force that sent her flying and the amazing excitement that welled up in her soul from experiencing such a touch from God! Now let me tell you what was happening in the angelic realm as God touched them. David, the pastor, got moved by the Holy Spirit with a word of knowledge and got lifted up from his seat by the power of God to deliver the message. The fire of The Holy Spirit was kindled as they all prayed for him. The Holy Spirit had His reason for pouring out His anointing. Power and fire shoot out of the person who is being moved by the Spirit. Within the spirit of David, a visible fire lit up inside of him and when he spoke the word apostle it shot out of his mouth and hands and actually hit each person. You can see this fireball flying towards each individual and when it hits their spirit and body and soul it pushes them over. It hits the spirit and sets their spirit on fire too. Like the tongues of fire at Pentecost this fire hits the body and the spirit of the person. Fire was shooting everywhere as he spoke the words that the Holy Spirit gave him. Pastor David was under the unction of the Spirit and he just stood up and did it. Everyone in its path got hit with the fire of God and got knocked off their feet. Lilly was overwhelmed. There were many angels who were there shining the Glory of the Lord. It was as if pure sunlight was shining everywhere in the room. The church actually was glowing with the clear brilliant white light that shined from each angel. Each person had their guardian angel by their side as the God of the universe chose to bless them. Marcos caught Lilly as she flew and grabbed hold of her body to keep it from hitting the ground with the force that sent her flying. Let's put it this way, Lilly went flying and Marcos flew with her and she fell on top of him to land on a soft floor rather than a hard floor. Marcos became the floor that Lilly landed on rather than the floor that was in the natural realm. He made sure she did not dash her foot against a stone floor. Just like the scriptures say. Angels were flying all over the place as the fire was hitting everyone. It was a most beautiful sight to see if you had the eyes to see it. Lilly, sorry to say, did not have her spiritual eyes open that day. She did feel the impact and the fire within her soul and spirit was burning. She wanted to run up to the rooftop and shout it to the world how much God loved everyone and how He sent His Son to save us! Lilly's prayer life after that grew even deeper than it was before as she was seeing God in many amazing ways use His Spirit to touch people.

On this day when Lilly was out praying she noticed a bunch of ravens in the woods behind her house. This land has been for sale for some time now and Lilly and her husband feel they are meant to buy it and build a safe haven place. She sees these birds gathering and crowing all over the place. They were coming from every direction to where all this commotion was going on. It was obvious the birds were excited. There had to be hundreds of them and all of a sudden they all took off together and flew away following each other. Lilly jumped up to see where they were going and they flew exactly to the end of her property and turned around in one mind and one accord and went right back to where they had been. The sound was loud and Lilly had never seen anything like this. She ran into the house to tell her husband and he just looked at her and had no interest in coming out to see. She felt a bit disappointed by his lack of response and only realized why later when he died. The story to come. The Lord showed Lilly that the birds represented people who were going to come because of The Holy Spirit and what was going to happen on that property. At the time Lilly did not realize that the birds did not leave the property line but stayed within the barrier of the land. This was showing Lilly that there was going to be a time when this property was where they would all be staying and not to even have to leave it. God gives messages to us in many ways. That was amazing to see how excited all these birds were. The excitement of the Spirit does the same thing for us as the children of God!

Lilly received a call that her mom was ready to die so she left to go to Florida where her mom lived. She met up with her sister and they flew together. They got there just in time because mom only lived another forty-five minutes after they arrived. Lilly felt moved to get into the bed next to her and talk to her. She knew it might have looked weird but she felt moved to tell her mom that they would take care of their step dad after she died. Lilly said, "mom we are here and it is alright for you to go home now. We will take care of dad for you." No sooner were the words spoken and her mom took her last breath. Lilly had years before mailed her a music tape with songs she had written and sung and her mom after listening to them told her it brought her back to her childhood in church. She began to go to church again and connected to God. It was the dream she had after her father died where her dad had shown her to reach out to her mother to tell her the truth. Lilly had, on more than one occasion, told her mom the way into heaven was through Jesus. She believed she was saved. This was another moment in time when Lilly spoke of the time to go home and death came right after. She was beginning to see the connection with her prayers and death and life. It was just too many times for them to be coincidences and she was realizing that God must have given her some kind of an anointing for it.

One night Lilly was sound asleep. She had what she thought was a dream but was actually a visitation. Let me explain what I am trying to tell you happened. There was a family member who was a distant relative from her husband's side of the family. Lilly was very concerned about his salvation because he was not what you would call a Christian. Lilly could not get him off of her mind but her husband at this time had major back issues so a trip there was kind of out of the question. That night Lilly found herself in his hospital room. She could see all these demons around him tormenting him and she could see their faces. There is no other way to explain what they looked like except they were dark black beings with gremlin-type faces and evil eyes that looked at you as if they wanted to devour your very soul. Lilly stood in the room as they all raged around the room in a frenzy. Lilly got so scared and found herself waking up taking a very deep breath. She was still in this what I call a trance-like state when she heard The Holy Spirit tell her, "you know you have to go back." Lilly already knew this in her soul because she had not done what she needed to do. The Spirit sensed her fear and put a supernatural peace upon her. He also rose up within her and gave her a boldness that she needed to go back with into what she called the pit of demonic rage and insanity. She could feel what those beings were feeling and it was insane. It was actual insanity operating and just doing its insane thing without any thought. Death and cancer and all the angry feelings he personally had joined together with these life-sucking creatures. It was like getting a taste of hell but Lilly knew hell was so much worse than this. She didn't even want to think what hell was like if this was just a few of the beings that would be there. It really was almost unbearable to deal with in her emotions. Picture being in a room with about twelve men who were so full of hate and all they wanted to do was just take it out on you. This was the feeling and she could actually feel their hate. Lilly not sure of how this was all happening ended up back in his hospital room. This time, she just stood there and all the creatures stopped what they were doing and stood at attention not moving or doing a thing. The person on the bed looked at Lilly. She wondered if he remembered who she was since she only met him a few times in life. That did not matter to her. What mattered was what she was about to say. He looked at her and she looked at him while all the spirits were quiet enough for him to hear her and only her. Lilly said, "you need Jesus!" He looked at her in confusion because he did not understand the salvation message and obviously went his whole life without knowing what Jesus had done for him and the rest of us. Without him saying a word Lilly could see humility in him as this disease had taken a man with a lot of pride and brought him down to this humble state. She then spoke out loud once again, "you cannot get into heaven without Jesus. "That is how it works." Without a word he bowed his head in humility and shook his head as if to say I understand. With that, Lilly was back in her room at her house, gasping once again as she took a breath and came out of this dream or trance. She really had no idea what had actually happened but she knew it was real. The phone call came the next morning that he had died in the middle of the night right after Lilly had gone to him and told him what he needed to do to get into heaven. When he shook his head with total humility he accepted the sacrifice of the Lord for his life. While he was alive he was most miserable and nasty and not a very loving man. We think some of these things we go through in this life are mean but I tell you what I believe to be true. Without this disease bringing this man to his knees he would have never made it in. God in His mercy allows the evil one to do certain things for His greater purposes. When we can actually grab that truth we stop taking this life on a personal level and realize this is the battleground between God and the devil and there are those in the army of the Lord and those who are not. Lilly had been recruited from a child and was becoming more of a warrior all the time. Not by power and not by might but by my Spirit says the Lord. We can be weak but He is strong. He will equip us with whatever we need when we need it. He will show us things to come to be prepared too if we learn how to listen. The spirit world around us is alive and well and functions all the time. Lilly was beginning to see clearer and clearer into this realm.

6. What If I Take Him Home?

This chapter will be by far the hardest chapter to write in the life of this emerald-eyed beauty. I want to make sure I leave nothing out of her story because as you can see it is a story to be told and a witness to the Father up in heaven. Is Lilly really so special? Some may say she is beautiful and some may say she is not. What bears witness in this life? If enough people say something we kind of take it at its word. That does not necessarily mean it is truth. Lilly never really thought of herself as beautiful, even though she heard it her whole life. She just lived her life like everyone else did accept she was truly in love with God and all she ever really wanted to do from the time she realized who Jesus was, was to serve Him and do whatever God wanted her to do. She had her weakness but never focused on her own will. She fell on her face in life just like we all do but God had His mercy on her and His favor was on her. All the blessings that God gave her along with His Holy Spirit and all these unbelievable things that happened stem from that. When I say, God, I mean Jesus too because Jesus point blank said that He and the Father were one. If that's the case, then you cannot truly love God without believing in Jesus. Some may disagree, but that is not up to me to decide, so I am off the hook with that. Now that we know Lilly was not this loud mouth self-seeking person who looked in the mirror and admired her own beauty let's read and see what was next in her life. Let me say this too at this point in the story. If we really love God and really follow Jesus we have to accept things that we may not want to or even desire too. Lilly was about to get asked the hardest question she would ever have to answer.

Lilly began to get a sense in her soul that another love was going to come into her life. Her husband was now unable to walk around because his back was so bad. He had been suffering for years. This one particular night when Lilly felt this love for someone who she did not know she felt The Holy Spirit tell her another love was coming into her life. She kicked the thought away because she was deeply in love with her husband and had no idea how that would ever happen. She knew she would never cheat on him. Her story of how she met her husband is in her book called

"Maybe Tomorrow" and it is one of anguish. This feeling of love, for whoever this person was, only happened once and then life went on and Lilly forgot about it.

Now the question comes from the Father up in heaven. Lilly was in the room by herself just lying on the bed and out of nowhere she hears within her spirit, "what would you do if I take David home?" We are using the name David for now for her husband but that was not his real name. Lilly just laid there thinking about the question and is this really God talking to her. Lilly responded rather quickly without having to even think very long about it. She answered back with "what would I do Lord?, you are the one who created all things and will I come against your decision to take him home?" She thought in her mind that if God was going to take him home He must have a good reason for it because Lilly knew He would not do anything to hurt her. She then said to Him, "you know what will happen to me." She meant that she would fall apart and there was no explanation needed because God knew very well how much she loved him. That was the entire conversation. There was only one person Lilly shared this with and it was her daughter who had witnessed her brother coming back to life that day in the hospital. Lilly kept this to herself and wondered what God's decision was going to be.

Time went by and Lilly and her husband were both going through some physical trials. Lilly had to take over doing everything because her husband could no longer stand up without severe pain. She was not thrilled about this because she worked very hard doing daycare and Lilly was not really feeling very well either. She was having trouble with her stomach and was relating it to irritable bowels from the stress of her husband being sick. I was further along in my writing but had to come back to this part of the book because after speaking with a family member of Lilly I realized there was much more involved in this part of her life than I first observed. If you remember the demon falon had a mission to destroy Lilly. He was not very successful in his attempt to use her beauty against her because Lilly was just too humble and too honest and obeyed the rules for the most part. The devil was sick of her at this point and her many times of prayer against his demons. He had to gather together once again his legion of these beings that left heaven and also the demons that had no bodies anymore after the flood of Noah. The demons from the flood were those who were born of women on the earth during that time and were called men of renown in the bible. They were part human so their desire is to be around people so they can be functioning again in a body rather than just floating around.

The meeting has been called into session. satan himself stood in front of all of them and they bowed before him. If they had not bowed down, they would have been tormented for their disrespect of their king. satan had the power to cause much pain to anyone he targeted to destroy. he still had to accept that God Almighty was more powerful than he was and had to submit to the will of the Father whether he liked it or not. There was a plan made to step in and be done with Lilly, her husband and the rest of the family. A few demons with some skill would get this job done for sure. It was all allowed for one reason and for one reason only. This suffering that was allowed was to create a new level of obedience for Lilly, to mature her, for the necessary tasks she was needed to do for the Lord. Her abilities in the spirit realm would excel during all the devastation she was about to go through. It was all so she could help the members of God's family. Nothing personal at all but for the glory of God. That is how it is down here since the fall of man. It is what it is, not because God wanted it this way but because man did not listen creating a world of evil to deal with. God takes everything and uses it for His ultimate purpose and glory. Lilly's entire family was in on this attack and satan could not see how this could ever fail. It was a sure thing and he was quite confident he would take them all down. he was so sick of miss green-eyed lady and how those piercing eyes just set his rage off every time he was lurking around. Who would do the job and do it right? The husband of Lilly had a spirit of fear already keeping him bound up. Lilly was sent a demon of cancer to slowly kill her off while she watched her husband fall apart. Nobody knew anything that was going on so it was just the greatest idea and plan to shut them all up. The children would be attacked after the two of them died. "How great it is to be me", said satan. i am just so brilliant and my kingdom is prevailing as all these humans are too stupid to even have a clue about us. They fall right into our traps all the time because they are just uninterested in their God. They have no idea of this spiritual realm and they have no clue they are spiritual beings in their bodies. Ah ha! Ah ha!", he laughed! After his episode of pride and self-indulgence of his boasting, he glared into the darkness all around himself and pointed to parthen, smiter, and levian. Some of his most fearful and angry spirits. "Go forth my faithful servants and destroy, destroy, destroy this family and do not return unto me until the task is complete. Time is short and we have many souls to torment! Planet earth will submit to us and I will be worshiped one way or the other before the great and terrible day of the Lord comes." With those words, they all screamed and trembled in fear and some shook so much you would have thought they were going to die. There was no death for spiritual beings, just torment and being bound up, never to deceive the world again or hurt any of the children of God for all of eternity. The day will come for Lilly and all those who are suffering, because of their love for the Lord, to come to an end. With a shout, Jesus will come and make war against the evil and stop him once and for all. Until that time, the children of God, like Lilly, will save as many people as possible by leading them to the truth about God and praying for healing for those who are hurting. From what we have just seen satan do, by sending out his top demons, it sure looks like Lilly and the rest of the family are not going to make it out alive.

We know Lilly has cancer but is unaware. I have to tell you what was happening to Lilly because if it were up to her, nobody would find out. I do not want to make her out to be out of the ordinary but what she was dealing with and the fact that nobody really knew that she was dying shows you how blessed she really is. The inward suffering, she was going through was just not tops on her list, everyone else was and that is The Spirit of God in her. She began to lose weight very quickly because no matter what she ate her stomach would get upset. The food was not passing through the digestive tract the right way because a tumor was growing and blocking the flow of things. Lilly associated all of her distress with irritable bowels because she was stressing over David. When she would have to go to the bathroom she would have severe pain in her lower intestines and she really didn't realize that the waste was being blocked from coming out the right way creating all the pain. She was only eating potatoes and bouillon soup because anything else made her feel nauseated. I am telling you this because we have to get a picture of Lilly and her faithfulness as a wife and her self-denial. She would fall to the floor in the bathroom in pain and never say a word to David because she did not want to put any more pressure on him than he had. At night she would sit on the side of the bed feeling so ill. She really did feel like she was dying but kept thinking it was all stress related and the pain she felt was her system just being upset from all she had to deal with. She had taken on all of David's workload too because he could not walk without pain. She would pray to God and ask Him to help her feel better. Lilly was slowly dying and did not even know it. She had to keep going because there was nobody else to do the chores, so even though she felt very weak, she pushed her body to the point of exhaustion almost every day. She was not getting the nourishment she needed and she was so tired. It was her sheer will to keep on going to make sure David was being taken care of. She cried many tears during this time but David never saw any of them. Marcos, her guardian angel, was constantly giving her words of inspiration and she could feel the energy that was being generated towards her. She knew there was some extra spiritual help that was motivating her. Lilly could barely cope but remained strong because of her faith and for David who was in his own time of struggle. He was in pain all the time and he battled with fear. Both of them were going through their own sufferings and slowly were drifting apart as they suffered in silence. David is dealing with these physical issues but not really sure what is happening to him either.

The fear demon has been there for many years now in his life and Lilly just reaches out to David with the spirit of love. The fear demon had been suppressed for the most part and that was the will of the Father so David could do the work of the Lord rather than stay bound up and not functioning because of it. Meeting Lilly whose anointing is to bring life to others helped him stand up again in his life, after the devil put such fear on him he was bound to his room. The love she showed him made him accept life again and not look at life as such a threat to his existence. He realized there was a reason and a purpose so he began to come back to life after feeling the need to hide from life in his room. Perfect love casts out fear the bible tells us. Her love that generated the love of God was being ministered to him daily and he received inner strength. He never got totally free because Lilly and David just did not know at this time that Christians could have demons too. That does not mean possessed it means oppressed from the outside. In other words, they come and hang around to influence. Angels of God influence people and angels of satan influence people. God's angels help us to feel good but the demons pull us right down and out of the will of God for our lives. Few people actually can see this realm. Lilly is one of the children of God who do. We have been given a glimpse here of this spiritual side and what the evil one set up for their family. We can see what the enemy's plan is so let's move on and see what actually happened. Battles go on daily in our personal lives so let's watch and see what miss green eyes actually has to go through. It is mind blowing. Do not forget this is based on a true story and that is what is so amazing about all of this.

David was feeling not quite right this one day and told Lilly he was not breathing correctly. Lilly had dealt with him for years thinking he was going to die because of fear so every time he would tell her he felt like he was going to die it was fear based and not actually any physical thing that was going to kill him. The fear would pass and he would then be fine. When he began to tell Lilly he was not breathing right Lilly watched to see what was happening. He jumped up and began to panic as he was gasping for air. Lilly called 911 and he had to be rushed to the hospital because he could not breathe. It was smiter coming in for the kill and Lilly watched his eyes roll back into his head as he was dying from lack of oxygen. Lilly thought to herself, "is he going to die? Is the Lord going to take him now from me?" The hospital he ended up in was not equipped to take care of David so he had to be sent to a better hospital that was more equipped to deal with him. He had to be incubated and on a machine that would pump the oxygen into his lungs and this hospital was just not set up for this. He was transported and Lilly had to follow by car. The entire family was battling with fear so there were a few of these demons mentioned that were creating an atmosphere of panic. Lilly kept praying and knew what the Lord had said to her the year earlier. He ended up in the IC unit for a few days and the diagnosis was heart issues and the lungs were filling up with fluid. He came home in a few days after recuperating and had to follow up with a heart doctor. Lilly thought, "is this it, Lord? Is my husband going to die, Lord?" There was no answer!

The very day that pastor David went into the hospital a new member of the church showed up. Lilly was at the hospital and the people were excited about this person who came out of nowhere to join the church family. This man played guitar and sang so he joined the music ministry with Lilly and the others. Lilly was losing weight very quickly during this time and felt good about it because she had gained too much weight anyway. Even though her stomach was not quite right she kept on going because there was too much to do. She had pain but again associated it with the stress in her life. Now let's see the demonic side of all this. The secret creepy things were killing the both of them without them even knowing it. We know all about the meeting where three were chosen to seal the deal of death. Poor emerald-eyed Lilly, all she wanted to do was serve the Lord and she really did work beyond her physical capability by pushing herself daily to finish all that needed to get done and then some. She was a go getter and had now taken on all of her husband's duties too because he was unable to walk without severe pain from a back injury. He also had this heart situation to deal with and the whole breathing issue that put, even more, fear on him. His fear of death was now a reality as he barely made it out alive with this last ordeal. They found out her husband had a growth in his lung and a heart blockage. He had severe allergies creating breathing problems along with the heart condition. You see these beings come in when we have no idea and just destroy when they can. During all of this, her husband started to pull back from her and suffered much in silence. He started backing out of the relationship so it would be less traumatic for Lilly. He felt he was going to die and wanted Lilly to go on so I believe he was quietly becoming more and more silent. He did not talk much at all and was very fearful but did not say a word to Lilly. Lilly too was suffering in silence when she would feel so sick. It got to the point all she could eat was chicken bouillon and a potato or else she would feel sick to her stomach. She was so focused on her husband who had now been in the hospital two times not being able to breathe. He had a stent put in his heart to open up the blockage and Lilly thought he was good to go. She believed God was not going to take him home at this point. Meanwhile, The Spirit was telling her she had cancer and she kept ignoring it because she was just too busy taking care of business. She was not really sure who was telling her but she kept rebuking it each time she felt it. There was no way she could have cancer she thought. She was a Christian who walked in the gifts so how would that even happen? The devil comes to steal, kill and destroy, seeking whom he may devour. Lilly had no idea. She went to church every Sunday and sang and preached because her husband could not stand up much.

One day her husband mentions to her that the new member of the music group was a lot like him. In other words, he was telling Lilly that this man was similar to her husband in personality. Lilly wondered why he said it but took no thought. Then a conversation came up about the fact that Lilly could not be alone. Her husband told her that God was going to bring someone into her life when he died. Lilly got angry that he was talking about dying. She did not want to even think of that. The subject was dropped. This is where things get really freaky and you might not even believe it but once again I assure you it did really happen just like I am telling you.

During one of their prayer meetings, Lilly gets what is called a word from the Lord for someone. This someone just happened to be the new music guy who has now been in the church for a year. By the way, may I say at this point, that he was very much in love with a woman who had left him. How do I know this? He had asked Lilly to pray for him about getting back together with her. Lilly gets this message for him from the Lord as a word of knowledge and tells him that God is going to send a woman into his life that is going to love him just for himself and he was going to be so blown away by this relationship. Lilly felt so happy for him after she told him this because she knew how sad he had been over the break up with this woman who he was engaged to at the time she left. After Lilly is done telling him this word from the Lord she hears within her spirit, "you are the woman." Lilly wanted to die because she felt she had given him a wrong word from the Lord because she could not be the woman. She was married to the pastor David so it must have been a false message. She felt terrible and had no idea why she would even think such a thing. She had no feelings for this man and was actually praying for him about this woman he was in love with. She kicked it to the curb as a blunder and felt bad but did not say a word about it to anyone. This same night during the prayer meeting the man who Lilly gave the word to walks up to the pastor, Lilly's husband, and tells him of a dream that he had last night. He had no clue what the dream meant but the pastor got the interpretation immediately when he told him. Pastor and this man who we will call the musician were Star Trek fans. This was a Star Trek type dream where there were two ships. In the dream, the music guy who is a captain transports to the pastor's ship who is also a captain. The musician's ship then blows up. He is watching the pastor, the captain of his ship, making soup. This is what Lilly's husband has always said he was going to do when he met Jesus. He was going to make Him a pot of soup. This has real meaning to it as the pastor is listening to this dream. He was cooking fennel in the pot and the music guy tells him he has to boil it. Fennel is a vegetable that the pastor recognizes very well so again it singles him out as the one captain in this dream. As the other captain, the musician, he then sees the pastor going off to the harvest to be with the Lord. He sees a woman walk away from the grief of losing her husband, the captain, without being destroyed by the grief. After he finished telling the pastor the dream the pastor tells the music guy that he is the other captain of the ship who comes over to his ship. Have you listened to what just happened here? Most amazing and God certainly has our steps divinely ordered. The musician had the dream of the pastor dying and him coming into the picture but has no idea what the dream is telling him. The pastor has been given another confirmation that God is going to take him home. Lilly was just told she was going to be the woman who comes into this musician's life by The Holy Spirit and the musician is told in a God-given dream that he was going to take the place of her husband who was going home. Lilly, the wife of the pastor, is the woman in the dream who does not fall apart after he dies. All three of them were shown that night what God was going to do. The only one who actually got it was the pastor. This man came on the first day pastor went into the hospital because God sent him to not only take over the church but to marry the pastor's wife so she will not be alone and fall into despair. Are you serious?

111

The only one who had any clue about what was going on was the pastor, Lilly's husband, who tried to tell Lilly about the dream but she had no interest in it. Her only focus at this point in time was to take care of her husband and had no intentions of even thinking he was going to die. The demons who were on the job of kill and destroy have now heard that God is intervening on behalf of Lilly. They become very enraged because part of this destruction plan is to devastate Lilly by the death of her husband along with cancer. The more emotional human beings become the more vulnerable they are to sickness and disease. Lilly's immune system because of watching her husband suffer for years with fear and pain had messed her up too. If she is not going to fall apart after he dies the demon's plan just might fail. This cannot happen because satan will surely rip them apart. They had to really come up with a sure plan in this or failure was eminent. They closely watched the situation to see what God was going to do in this. They really had no idea except for the dream they heard. They would wait and if anyone else had to be attacked to bring down this ministry and the work of God, not a problem, they would just call a few fellow demons to come and help up the power. Fear, anger, and trauma are a few of the most dangerous weapons of the devil. All having to do with our emotions. So sad and yet so real! Lilly was about to get side swiped and had no clue.

Lilly sat one day on the couch and David looked at her from across the room and finally opened up with what he believed God was showing him and said, "Lilly, I am going to die." Lilly could not accept what he said and got angry. You would think Lilly would have remembered what the Lord had said to her but she was in denial. He stared at her intensely and again told her he was going to die. She could see he was serious and took what he said to heart but neither said another word and they left it at that. Lilly wondered if he was right this time, because he had felt so many times before when he would have a panic attack that he was dying, but it was only intense emotions of fear. This time, it was not said in a panic but was said with an assurance that it was going to happen. Lilly would not even allow herself to think about it. She knew she could not deal with it and she did not go there in her thoughts. He was not able to preach very much because he could not breathe right or stand without pain, but the day after he told her those upsetting words he preached after not being able to for weeks. This one Sunday which happened to be Palm Sunday, he just was given the ability to preach. After the service, they came home and David cried to Lilly saying how thankful he was that he was able to preach one more time. Lilly heard what he said about being able to preach one more time as if he was not going to be around much longer. Once again Lilly realized how convinced he was that his time was up. Within two days he was rushed to the hospital because he could not breathe. As he was fading because of the lack of oxygen he threw her a kiss and waved goodbye. This was right before he went into a coma. Lilly watched and her soul got hit with the reality that he was possibly right and he was not coming back to her. She felt ill and her mind could not even deal with what was happening. She looked up and asked, "are you taking him home Lord?" It was the hardest thing Lilly ever had to go through. Just watching him laying on that hospital bed as if he were sleeping with no real life to him was so sad. Lilly kept going over to him and speaking in his ear that she was not going to let him stay like that with all these artificial machines keeping him alive. The doctors tried to see if his brain activity would improve but it did not. He was either going to remain a vegetable or they would have to allow God to do whatever His will would be. Lilly felt he was going to die at this point but she still held out for a possible miracle to happen. She had seen people on their death beds come back to life more than once but this time, she had been spoken to by God when He asked her what would she do if he was to go home. She usually got a knowing about whether a person was going to die or live since her gift had to do with life and death. Watching her husband who she was so very much in love with was a whole different story.

While I am writing this I just remembered another miracle of life and death where Lilly was used by God. It happened to be another coma situation where a young teenager had a car accident and was in a coma. Lilly and her husband went to pray for him and when they showed up they stood on either side of the bed. They grabbed his hands and told him they were there and Lilly felt him squeeze her hand. She was stunned but realized he actually heard them but could not move. He was trapped in his body. Lilly began to speak to his soul words of life and then

113

commanded him to come out of the coma and they left. After being in a coma for some time he woke up and was healed right after the prayer. Watching her husband made her remember this young man but Lilly still did not feel her husband was going to wake up. She did not know why he would have to die but she remembered God telling her, "what if I take him home?" She surrendered to the will of God. She also remembered the second time he was in the hospital there was a young man who also had a car accident and had been in a coma for over a month. Lilly felt so bad for the family but did not even think to pray for him because she was so wrapped up in her emotions with her husband being in the intensive care unit too. Her beautiful son, the one who was born dead and came back to life said to Lilly, "mom we need to pray for him." Lilly was so moved by the compassion of her son even though his father was lying in a bed down the hall. He cared enough and obviously was getting moved by The Spirit. Lilly said, "let's pray." and they both walked in front of the glass pane that he was behind, laying there so lifeless. Lilly watched her son pray and she backed him up and commanded him to come out of the coma. This is true and may I say unbelievable! He woke up right after the prayer and the family was so excited. Lilly had to tell them that God did it because of prayer. The glory had to go to the Lord because they had no idea that Lilly and her son had even prayed. With all the amazing miracles of death to life that Lilly had seen she still knew her husband was going home. May I say this too. Lilly in her selflessness knew in her heart that her husband was done with this life. He was tired of suffering in his body with all the pain and he was so in love with Jesus that it was meant for him to now be able to meet his Lord face to face. Out of love for her husband, Lilly let him go in her heart knowing that this was the will of God for him. After being in a coma for a week he died. I have to just add this because we have talked about all these impy creatures that come to destroy us but I also want to tell you that every time Lilly was in the intensive care unit she could feel the presence of God. She could feel all the angels of God that were there to comfort all the children of God who were suffering in their flesh. There was a peace that you could not explain except the fact that there were angelic powers and forces beyond our physical realm. She could see them in her mind with their white shining presence of the light of God. They just permeated the entire place with the peace of God from their presence. A woman came in and went from room to room playing her harp one day while the people were in bed trying to recuperate from whatever sickness or accident they had. The music was soothing and comforting to all the souls who were there. This was the same place where the younger man had been in a coma for a month and came out of it right after Lilly and her son prayed. There definitely was God, in the midst, of all the suffering souls. Figure that out! The only thing I can say is God tells us in His word that nothing can separate us from the love of God which is in Jesus. Neither death nor life, nor any demonic being, nothing can take the love of God from us. We have the choice to believe it or not! Lilly believed it and even though she was devastated by God's decision she trusted He had another plan for her future.

The whole time God had been showing the pastor, before he died, what he was going to do with the church and his wife. He so gracefully accepted the will of the Lord and knowing that Lilly would not have to be alone. His concern was for her and he would tell Lilly all the time that she was not going to be alone if he ever died. Lilly would never get into the conversation because it was just too upsetting for her to even think about it. During this time when he was so sick, he told Lilly that if the musician called for prayer that he did not want her to talk to him. He told her he would talk to him. Lilly thought that because the musician was single and had been hurt by some woman that David did not want to put him in a situation where he might fall for Lilly. Things like that can happen so easy when we are vulnerable. You really have to be careful. Lilly knows now that he wanted to make sure nothing would happen before the time because he was the only one who knew what God had planned at this time. In his love for Lilly, he was willing to let her go so she could continue in her life to fulfill her mission. Lilly did not see any of this until way after he died. She then put two and two together and remembered the feeling of another love coming into her life. The word she got at the prayer meeting about the woman coming into the musician's life came back to her and she was in awe at God's choice to tell them all what was going to happen. Lilly was in awe that the Holy Spirit had actually told her she was going to be part of his life and love him. The Star Trek dream she only really heard after the musician told her one day and she remembered her husband trying to tell her and she ignored him. She felt bad about it when she realized what the dream was actually saying, but she knew it was not meant for her at that time to totally understand. Lilly also found out that the musician had another dream of the pastor drowning and that is what happens when your lungs stop working and they fill up with fluid. There was a lot of demonic working in the flesh but God uses it all for His greater purposes. If we knew the half of what was going on in this spirit realm we would be able to rebuke most of it and get free. Since only a few Christians are even aware of it; we remain in the dark. Lilly for many years did not really have a clue. She suspected but did not know that even Christians can have these demonic beings come into their lives and create torment. Her husband suffered for many years with fear and if Lilly would have really known it was a spirit she could have prayed for him to be free. Many nights he would have panic attacks and vent out all these fears even though he really knew the truth in his heart about the love of God. One night Lilly actually watched this demon manifest right in front of her. She got angry at what it was doing and could not say anything to her husband so she just told it to be quiet. He thought she was talking to him but right after it was rebuked it did shut up. Lilly knew that this could possibly be a demon but was not really sure. Her husband had no idea and I do not think he believed it possible. Some may be creeped out by all this but this realm exists for real and they need bodies to function the way they need to. They really do not have the right to our bodies and we have to tell them to get lost in the name of Jesus. Many afflictions stem from demonic beings that latch on and become the affliction because that is what they are. Cancer is a demon and Lilly had one inside killing her slowly while she dealt with all the issues her husband was going through. There was no time for Lilly to stop and even think about what she was feeling. It was a good thing but then again it was not because the more Lilly ignored her symptoms the larger the demon grew and death was imminent. Before we go into this part of the story I have to tell what happened after the pastor died. I wonder at this point what you are actually thinking? So many amazing things that Lilly watched happen that it almost seems surreal. It is all true and yet Lilly never thought who she was. Lilly actually has to realize that she is one of God's anointed. She still thought of herself as just like everybody else. Lilly, you are not like everybody else. Miss green-eyed, emerald-eyed, woman of God, you must recognize that God has called you to do these marvelous and awesome miracles of the Lord. Find joy in it and spread the good news!

Lilly left the hospital to take a breather from just sitting there watching her husband in this coma. She could not take it anymore. Her heart was broken and every time he would yawn they thought maybe he was waking up, but he did not. It was just this waiting for death to occur, or hopefully life, and the not knowing that was driving her crazy. Lilly truly felt that if it were not for the help of the Holy Spirit she would have really lost it. She was barely coping at all. Each day Lilly would call the musician who she had asked to help her get through this. She knew he had lost the woman he loved and had an understanding what Lilly was going through. She was updating the church by letting him know what was happening to their pastor. She went home to collect her thoughts and begin preparing for the worst. She spent the one night after being in a motel for almost a week and was going to go back the next day. The decision was made by the family to take him off of life support so it was only a matter of time and Lilly did not really want to watch him gasping for air. Her love for him was so deep she did not feel the need to just sit there and watch death take the love of her life away. Even though she really did not want to be there she was going to go back anyway because it was just what you do when someone dies, you sit and wait. Death was still hard for her to deal with and she had said goodbye to him. She was going to go back because it had to be done, but it was not what she really wanted to do. She had been getting the church ready for the funeral so she stopped over there before she was going back. His daughter called from the hospital and said no need to come back they say he will not last much longer. Lilly stayed at the church preparing. While she was walking toward the front of the church she stops dead in her tracks and says, "is that you?" She meant her husband. Lilly knew he was standing right in front of her and she abruptly stopped. The mind then tells you no way, this cannot be real. She began talking with him as if she could see and hear him even though the voice was not audible and what she saw was in her mind's eye. He told her, "I had no idea I was in a coma for a week. I am sorry you had to go through that." Lilly paused for a minute as she could sense he was not really showing any emotions for what she had been going through. He was different in his emotional response to her suffering. It was as if it was normal and this was the way it was. Her husband was very close to her and did not want her to be alone so his lack of concern for where she was at was unusual to her. She also knew that he was a spirit so things are different with the emotions on the other side. She was wondering at this point, is he dead and is coming to me? He quickly told her he was giving her his mantle for ministry and she thought, is that all he is concerned about when he is dying on me or has died. It was all he was concerned about from the other side because that was the main issue, the ministry and the word of the Lord. He knew and Lilly also knew it but she was an emotional basket case right now and he just seemed so indifferent to what was happening to her. She did understand though because on the other side there is no sadness just the reality of God and what is going on in His kingdom and the purpose for life. As she was thinking of what she knew he was telling her the phone rang and she ran to get it. Sure enough it was his daughter telling her that her father had just died a few minutes ago. Lilly had her confirmation that he was dead and she knew now that he was really there and was actually communicating with her. She went into another room where she could be alone and then asked him if there was anything else he had to tell her. He then said, "This was not my will but the Father's will, timing is very critical." Lilly knew what he meant by that. She knew God took him home because he could no longer do what was necessary to finish the mission for God and since the coming of the Lord is soon things have to get done. God stepped in to take him home so the ministry could move forward. Lilly had peace in knowing God made this choice but she was still so messed up right now. He then said, "Don't worry about money and it is all good, it is all good." Lilly thought what an odd thing to say when she was a basket case but she did know what he meant. In other words, God had it all planned out and she had nothing to worry about. That was all she heard and again she could not help but notice that he

118

was unemotional about it. How could we have any joy in heaven if we go there and are so disturbed about our loved ones we are freaked out. There is complete peace because they know the end result of all the suffering that we go through. Lilly could feel the lack of concern for her and I have to say it bothered her a bit because she was in turmoil and he didn't even acknowledge it. That was not like her husband and she truly knew at that moment in time he was gone from her life. There was no sharing her hurt soul with him because he was not even on the same level of emotion that she was on. People cry out to their loved ones when they leave because of their own upset feelings and they think the relative who left is relating to them on a personal level. That is just not true. Once we leave this realm and become spirit we really do become like the angels. There is no more marriage, no more sexual desires, and as far as feelings and emotions go they do not operate by feelings at all. They perform their duties and the emotions are there but very much a non-motivating factor in how they serve God. Command and action is what they live by. Emotion is the very tool the devil uses to mess us up because most of the time we go by our emotions and that is our downfall. Feelings should not control us. The Spirit of God should be what we follow, not what we want to do and feel we need to do. When we leave here we are so different in that respect and it is actually a freedom not to feel all these negative emotions. Can you imagine living life without having to deal with fear and anger and loneliness, etc. Tell me am I not correct in the fact that we are pretty much controlled by our emotions down here? This family came apart because of emotions that were running so high that it became everyone's motivation factor. Everyone was in their own brokenness and dealing with it their own way. Hurt feelings began to excel and even though nobody had intentions of hurting anyone, everybody played a role in creating a family that ended up being ripped apart. Lilly's husband who had many fears before he died had this conversation with her and had nothing but peace while he was telling her what God had done and why. He spoke as if all he had to give her was the information he needed to share. Lilly felt some peace after he spoke to her at that moment because she had been given some answers. It did disturb her that there was no real interaction with him on a personal level. The love of her life was

119

gone. There would be no more oneness the way she needed it and it hit Lilly. She got a bit angry that he had left her behind but she was happy for him because she knew he was alright and with the Lord. Free! He told Lilly it was all good so now what was in store for Lilly after he told her it was all good? It was hard for her to grasp that he was telling her it was all good when in fact he had just died on her and left her. She knew it was from a spiritual aspect but still it seemed a bit cold to her. All good she thought, "I feel like I am going to die and my husband is telling me it is all good." These words and the unemotional way they were spoken to her actually helped miss green-eyes face the truth that he was really gone and there was no more earthly connection to him. The marriage was really over and the saying until death do us part really fit as far as Lilly was concerned. It hurt because her husband was not only dead he was unemotionally detached from her. When people feel they can never remarry because they feel so guilty thinking their loved one will feel upset. That is so far from the truth. They could care less because the place where they now exist does not need any companionship at all. They are filled with the fullness of the Lord and are in need of nothing. Lilly felt that from her husband. On earth while he was alive he very much needed her support and love and reassurance all the time. He was different on the other side and Lilly felt a bit offended by it. She would have to say she actually felt a bit rejected by the whole death thing. She shut the door to her feelings and looked up to God, even though she did not like His decision, and told herself if her husband just told her that his death was all good then there just had to be something in store for her that was going to replace this loss in her life. She walked away feeling lost and broken and in desperate need of love. Nobody knew how she really felt because she could not even share this moment with them. The family would just think she went nuts which they all ended up thinking anyway. She had been a Spirit-filled pastor for a long time and with the gifting that Lilly had it was hard to share many things. The decision to even tell about the amazing things Lilly witnessed was done with much prayer and seeking the will of God. This book is being written because God said to write it. You have not seen the half of what happens with Lilly. The devil planned this whole situation right down to the timing of the development of cancer and the emotions involved. He hated her so much he had to use the very people that she loved the most in this life to take her down.

All hell broke loose in her personal life. The demons are in for the continued kill. Death was never meant to be but when it does happen God takes the spirit and soul with him or the devil sucks it into hell. Lilly and her son began to argue because Lilly had to keep busy so she went to the church and played music and hung out with the musician. The family all wanted her to help them deal and she could not. She had to put her husband to the side since he was gone and happy with the Lord and keep on going forward. She blocked all her emotions and tried not to be so lonely that she could not function. She asked everyone in the church to just be her friends so she could deal with this. She asked the musician if he would help her since he knew what it was like to lose someone you love. He said, of course, he would help her by being a friend to her. The people in the church really stepped up to help her. Her son was a loner type and just wanted Lilly to stay home like she did before with his father. This is the miracle son who Lilly spoke life back into. The devil wanted him dead too, remember? He was so broken too by the loss of his father. He was graduating in a few months from high school and dad who was his spiritual strength is now gone. Mom was running away to find her own help in this and her son felt abandoned by her. She kept reaching out to him and telling him if you need to talk I am here for you but there was no communication between them There never really was any communication. That was their downfall. They had never really had a relationship. Her son did his own things in life and so did Lilly. During this time when they really should have connected with each other Lilly was running to the musician. She did not want to deal with anybody's hurts because she could not even deal with her own. She loved her son dearly but every time when she was home around him he retreated to his room and she felt even more alone in her house. He felt like she was not reaching out to him and she felt the same way. She went to the only place she knew to find comfort, the church and the musician whose soft spoken words of encouragement touched her very soul. He was so comforting in his person because he came with such a peaceful mannerism that Lilly just felt peaceful around him. She also felt guilty because her son was just sitting home alone. He never told Lilly that he needed her to talk to him and she wanted to help him but did not know how. Her son, the loner, was not handling being alone very well right now and yet every time Lilly tried to talk to him but anger came out at her. Lilly tried to explain that she could not just sit and watch the television or she would die. Lilly could see the evil one stepping into the picture. Rage and anger began to come at Lilly because everyone wanted her to be their strength and she ran away from it all. The demons were lurking all around influencing because the strength of the household had died and Lilly was alone and vulnerable. Her son felt the need to take charge because his father had told him to watch out for his mother. He was trying to do so but became possessive in telling her what to do. She had to tell him to stop and the daily anger and tension was killing her. Lilly knew that all of this was demonic attacks. The entire family felt that Lilly was losing it at this time and yes Lilly was barely holding on but I have to say from watching this from the eyes of the Lord it was quite obvious who the demons were attacking. Lilly may have been running away from her grief but the anger that came back at her was relentless and the family turned on her because she was running to the musician for her help. Lilly understood they were concerned for her safety but they had no idea that it was all powered by demonic fear. The reason I know this is because Lilly was in the will of the Father. They were against what the real plan of God was in this because they could not see with their spiritual eyes. Everyone was convinced Lilly was moving way to fast and it just could not be God. Who was this musician anyway who has stepped into their mother's life? They had absolutely no confidence in the ability of their mother to discern what was God or what was not. Her son was told by his father, in fear, to watch over his mother and with that came control, fear, and anger when Lilly did what she felt to do. The time she spent at home was like a nightmare come to life. It became a vicious cycle of anger coupled with fear for her life. Nobody was in the peace of the Lord except Lilly. She was the only one who was not angry but was so wounded by the loss. Lilly could not deal with her son's anger and actually felt fear herself when he would come at her venting out this anger and telling her what she should be doing. She wanted to talk to her son but there was no talking anymore. Her son did not agree with her way of handling her grief. He wanted her not to go anywhere and just sit home. That would have been her death for sure. Lilly had to keep on moving forward and not dwell on anything that upset her during this time. Everybody else had plans to stay together and wallow in the sorrow that was trying to kill Lilly's soul. The demonic force of anger got more and more strength as Lilly refused to entertain it. She tried to tell her son that he had to stop blaming her for everything but he just would not understand where she was coming from in this. They all became very possessive in their need to protect Lilly. Instead of praying about what Lilly was doing they resorted to fear of what Lilly was doing. Lilly might have been grieving but she had not lost her mind like they felt she did. Fear and anger because the need to protect her was there and they all felt she was ignoring them. She was because her focus was on what God wanted. She kept telling them she was alright but nobody believed her. This was all not normal to them for her to keep running to the church. That was her only place of peace because playing music and talking to God was what she had to do. Sitting with all her children who had no idea that it was the will of God and all they wanted to do was feel bad was not what she was looking to do. God made His choice and Lilly although heartbroken was ready to move forward into the new will of God for her life. She heard it from her own husband after he died and how could she possibly share this with them when all they wanted was to never forget their father. Lilly did not want to forget their father, her husband, but unless she accepted her new life whatever it was she would lay down and die in depression. She was in survival mode and her heart was very upset for all her children who were grieving too. She could not make things right for any of them and watching her son who she deeply loved turn on her in anger was something she could not take. She could not help that the musician came into her life. It was not her plan but within her soul, she already knew that he was going to marry her because the Holy Spirit had already revealed it to her at the prayer meeting. She did not remember but she knew deep within so when the family came against him and her for this relationship it broke her heart again. What did they want her to do? Her son would not talk to her when she was home. He did not want her to go out and

123

leave him and yet he refused to talk to her when she was there. The problem was her falling for this total stranger and fear, fear, fear! Fear has torment and the evil one planned the attacks and they were working. The man of faith who they all looked up to was gone. Their mother who they also looked up to was gone in her emotions and was on the run, to where they did not know. What was lacking in all this was trust in God. God had let them all down by taking their father so what was left. Fear which had torment. evil will have his day but until he is bound up we either have to be spiritual enough to discern what is going on or be a pawn for the evil one to mess around with. All the fear and anger was justified by all because mom was being very inconsiderate and uncaring for her children. That was how they all felt so, therefore, mom had to be the one in the wrong even though mom was the only one listening to the will of God for everyone. Once the anger set in it was all over and nobody talked to Lilly again. She was left with the musician and those that stayed in the church after the pastor died. People actually left the church because of his death too.

Meanwhile, in secret, the cancer was growing. The family turned against her when they realized she was hanging out with the musician because they felt abandoned by her but Lilly loved them all very much. She was just trying to find her way with the plan of God for her life. Nobody was even thinking of what God's plan was in all this. They were too busy feeling sorry for themselves. May I say that what I just said is not being said as a put-down, it was just the way it was when he died. It happens to most families as the focus is usually on themselves rather than the deceased. Most people fall into the feel sorry thing instead of looking at the freedom for the person who was suffering. Lilly was not feeling sorry because she was a mature Christian who knew life had plenty of sorrows to deal with and God was the only answer to them all.

Lilly started to have these feelings for the musician but was very afraid of falling into some kind of trap because of her emotions so she was very skeptical of anything she really felt. Lilly would have to admit, though, that these feelings gave her a real sense of being alive again. She had been dealing with death for some time now and the new hope with this musician truly brought life to her soul! Everyone in the family told her she should not be hanging out with him. Her husband had just died and she was off the wall. She got angry because they had no idea what she was going through and she knew this was giving her life. It was not her fault her husband up and died and left her so who were they to tell her what she should do or not do. The anger from the family and Lilly would have to say, the demonic activity, excelled and everyone was so offended. Everyone was blaming Lilly for it. They wanted Lilly to comfort them. She could not and she was in survival mode. She did her best to bring peace to her son but he got so angry she had to tell him off and told him if he continued to do this to her he had to leave. She told him she had enough sorrow and could not handle his hatred towards her. Lilly knew it was a demon and could see it influencing him because he was so hurt too. They all felt she abandoned them and I guess she did in her own way because she had found comfort in a friendship sent by God and was clinging onto it for dear life. Nobody saw it that way. They only saw it as a betrayal to her husband. Lilly thought to herself, "he is dead, what is it they want me to do? Sit and dwell on it so I can fall apart." She was fighting to live.

The daycare she did for income had her grandchildren and many of her daughter's friends' children. They all took their children out including her daughter because of the musician. The excuse was that he might be crazy and we do not want our children around him. Nobody told Lilly the real reason they were taking their children out accept her daughter. Their lack of confidence in Lilly and her choice to make this man her friend was based on fear. Her daughter was upset and angry, so she walked away from Lilly, her mother. It was because they felt that Lilly did not care about anyone except herself at that time. Instead of the family praying to God and finding out what she was doing and that it was in the will of the Lord, they all went the route of fear and anger. This could just not be right they thought. What would make her want to see this stranger and not just stay with the family? They had no idea how critical timing actually was in the winding down of this world before the return of Jesus. God was moving quicker than anyone would have expected and what they did not realize was that love just does not happen that easy. If this was true love what would be the chances of it just happening or just maybe God was involved in it. Last time I remember death has no timing when it comes to our schedule in life so why should love have time to surface? Love is love and if Lilly was truly falling in love with this man how beautiful that she will not be alone. He did not fit into their plans so he was not supposed to be. Lilly was condemned by them all. She lost all her income because of this anger and fear and did anybody care that now they just put their mother in a financial collapse on top of the death of her husband. No, it was all about how Lilly hurt them all. As an outsider, I have to say they had no understanding of Lilly or her anointing from God. If they had really been part of her spiritual life none of them would have reacted the way they did. Lilly could have shared the story about what God was doing and they would have trusted in her and God. Lilly did share what the Lord was doing but nobody believed her and to this very day I do not think they ever really got the plan of God in this or the why. Can you see how dangerous it is when we do not walk in The Spirit? We miss the mark and we create all kinds of suffering for ourselves. The demons go crazy and we listen to them and the fear they put on us.

Lilly felt like Job especially when she found out she had cancer. She was feeling some joy because of the musician in her life and was beginning to see a plan. The musician got a word from the Lord and told her she was going to have a rough few days ahead of her but she would be alright. She asked what he meant by that and he said he did not know but that it was something they were going to have to go through but God said it would be alright. That was not what Lilly wanted to hear. During this time Marcos, her guardian angel was working overtime to keep reassuring Lilly that her life would be fine. He kept away the demons that were trying to make her give up and fall into despair. Between the angry spirits shooting at her from everywhere and the depression spirits he was chasing them away all the time. They were not permitted to latch onto Lilly. She had divine protection at this time because death in the form of cancer was growing inside her colon. Lilly lost sixty pounds during this stressful time and one day she felt the lump. She knew she had to call the doctor but did not really want to. She told him and he told her to go to the hospital. They found cancer but she was so numb already she just went with the flow. She was transported to a bigger hospital where they would do the surgery and remove the tumor. It was a fast moving situation and Lilly came out of the operation and recovered. While she was in the hospital, she witnessed to an elderly lady about the love of God. The musician saw the spirit of death on her and went and prayed and when he came back death had left Lilly. He did not share that with her until much later after she was feeling better. The demon went nuts, the one that was going to kill her. It took off like a bat out of hell and went off screaming. It knew the torture it was in for because of its failure. Lilly was not going to die from cancer after all. Who is this musician that has come into this picture to save Lilly? It was not in the plan of God to take Lilly home yet. There was much work to do. Death is gone but fear is trying to grab hold of Lilly at this point in time. She was so done with all this and she really felt like she knew what Job must have felt after losing everything.

Remember falon? The pervert demon. He still had his sites on Lilly to violate her. He and his demon friends of fear and anger were all there to influence the family. Anger was there from her family while Lilly went through all this sickness but they were at least still talking to her. She had all this love for everyone and could not understand why they were so angry at her. Everybody was looking at their own sorrow and yet Lilly was the one who had lost the most in this. Emotional upheaval can allow these beings to step right in and do the damage they are looking to do. falon knew Lilly was going to be very vulnerable in the hospital and not even alert enough to know what was going on. Her soul would feel the violation he was planning and he had waited long enough to stick it to her. He was thrilled at his chance to finally have just one moment in time where he could say I got ya. Fear tried to get her because the one night in the hospital Lilly could hear a demon screaming from the other room. She wondered if it was reacting to her being in the hospital. The whole ward heard this spirit screaming with this piercing sound of torment. Lilly could barely take it. It was so disturbing to her she wanted to run away and cry. She had enough pain and just wanted to feel normal again. Then she woke up with one of the nurses touching her chest and her eyes popped open as she looked up at her. The nurse immediately told her she was fixing her gown but Lilly did not feel that was the truth. She felt she was being violated by some pervert demon. She wondered how many times had she done this while she was asleep. Lilly felt so discouraged and now felt used by some woman nurse who was enjoying invading her privacy. She just wanted to go home. Home to what? A son who had hatred towards her and the loneliness of having no husband. In all these feelings she also knew God had saved her life and the tumor was very large and the doctor said she was stage three borderline stage four cancer. She was told to have chemo but felt not to do it. Lilly knew God delivered her. falon had his time of feeling satisfied but Lilly just brushed it off, what the nurse had done because she never really knew what happened. She asked God to heal any damage it might have caused her soul. Did falon succeed? It may seem like evil wins here but ultimately they will all go to hell forever.

The musician is what helped Lilly cope with all of it. Nobody was on her spiritual level accept the musician so there wanting her to turn to them for comfort could not have worked. This whole situation was so ordained of God that the only way to get it was to be able to listen to The Holy Spirit. They would have needed to be on a spiritual level that was compatible to where she was at. The whole death of her husband had been a spiritual move of God which nobody could accept but Lilly. Lilly knew through all the words given that God had brought the musician to town just to become her husband. God had said it to all of them including her husband who died. The devil was enraged by it because he knew a vision was given to her late husband many years ago and it was going to come to pass even though he was no longer here to do it. With the help of this man of God who was sent to be part of the ministry, this vision would be fulfilled. To stop God's plan, the demons would have to come up with a plan. What better way to do this than to convince Lilly that she was wrong and that God was angry at her and her late husband was mad at her. People in the church who wanted to step into the pastor's shoes came from all over. They made up stories about the musician just to put fear on Lilly to walk away. The family kept telling her he may be crazy or some evil person. Lilly was so full of everybody's opinions she was in confusion not knowing what to do. She just sat quiet and Marcos, her guardian angel, helped her get a focus on what was the truth. All Lilly knew at this point was that she felt this overwhelming love for the musician. She did not want to hurt anyone in the family but she had to follow what God was showing her was the future for her and the ministry. The Lord led her to the scripture verse about putting family above the Lord and how you would not be worthy of being His so she was following the Lord no matter what anyone felt or said. She was so broken especially when her son walked out the door after he realized Lilly was going to marry the musician. It was not that he was against this man, he felt betrayed, like they all did, by her moving so quickly forward. Lilly understood her son's feelings and she was very distressed about them, but Lilly knew that God was in on this. She had realized all the things that were said in the dreams and words of knowledge were God speaking and telling them what His plans were. The whole family walked out of her life during this time but Lilly knew she was in the will of the Lord so she just kept on going forward. She was so broken by the loss of her husband that this was just one more thing to have to deal with. Sometimes God makes moves that we do not understand but they are for the greater purpose and we must just blindly trust Him. To sum it up, Lilly, the chosen woman of God, just lost her husband to death. She herself had colon cancer and nearly died too. The entire family was not speaking to her anymore because of the musician. She lost her complete income and was about to lose her home too, without some kind of an intervention. The devil did succeed in one part of the plan to take down the family. demons were influencing all of them and they all fell into the trap of anger and hurt. Lilly loved them all but they all felt she dumped them when in fact they were all the ones who would not talk to her and judged her for what she did during her time of grief. Fear and trauma hit everyone and everyone suffered and there was no family left anymore for Lilly. She was called names and was hated for what they all said she did. What did Lilly do? She followed the leading of the Lord when nobody believed her enough to stop feeling she was disrespecting her husband who had passed away. They did not know he was telling her before he died that the musician was coming into the picture to rescue Lilly and the church from destruction and to make sure the vision would come to pass. The musician was the hero in this. Nobody else saw that he was the hero in all this but the devil sure did. Every means the devil could throw out at Lilly to stop this relationship, the enemy used. He used fear against Lilly by sending the demon whose name was parthen to hang around and whisper in her ear. She could actually discern the words he spoke. She heard over and over again, "You are not listening to The Spirit in this and you will screw up your life." Your whole family is against you and what you are doing, how can you possibly be right? Maybe this man is a psycho like they say he might be. What kind of love did you have for your dead husband when you so quickly are moving on? They are right you have betrayed him and do not care about anybody but yourself." All these words of accusation kept coming at her. She would ponder them all and then would go back to her true feelings for all of her children and her late husband and know they were words of condemnation and not truth. She had men in the church who were already interested in her. She actually looked great from losing the weight and felt good too after the cancer was gone. She had a real sadness though and could not shake it. Her life was surreal and her son was on her heart all the time because he walked out and was gone. His sisters stepped in to help him and that was what created much of their anger at their mother. His sorrow became their anger. Lilly tried to explain that her son leaving was not all her fault like they believed. They did not live with the hatred shooting at her and the disrespect. Lilly and her son ended up in a real anger match and Lilly too became very angry at him for his behavior and his lack of understanding as to where she was coming from in all this too. It seemed it was all about the children and their hurt. Lilly was just wrong and that was it. There was no compromise, just maybe, everyone played a part in it. Just maybe sorrow hit them all, and each one dealt with it in their own way, and that should be respected rather than to point the finger. There was plenty of condemnation going around, and fear. The musician was the only one with the clear head in all this. Lilly could feel his compassion when she would cry her eyes out over the loss of the family. Rejection was very much the feeling they all had including Lilly. All of it was based on fear. Lilly had episodes where she felt she could not deal, but the musician was always there to help her. I think part of the anger was that Lilly had found help and the rest were all floundering looking for someone to help them deal with this trauma. Why had God stepped in so quickly to rescue Lilly? If He had not Lilly would have died from cancer. The mission that her late husband had to accomplish was not done and it is vital. The vision he had been given was a place of peace where Christians were going to come and live in peace. He did not know the why for this place and he did not know the when either. The waiting for over thirty years made him weary because he really had no understanding what this vision was for. Lilly and the musician discover the why and the real reason for the wait. The story goes on and Lilly is about to move into this realm of the spirit like never before. In her humility, she always tries to see both sides of the story and she did see the children's side but she also knew things they did not. The imps were creating much turmoil in all of their lives and Lilly could see clearly. None of them had a clue they were battling with demonic beings that were commanded to break up the family and destroy this vision from ever happening. The angels from the Lord were also keeping very busy trying to counteract the negative input from these little nasty beings. You really do not want to see them like Lilly does. They look right at you especially when they know you can see them. They make faces at you and snarl at you and even smirk when they know you can't make them leave because the person likes the sin. I tell you the truth in this. What you are reading is the absolute truth of this world of the demonic and the angelic that are functioning around people all the time. There are voices to be heard. Your own voice. The voice of the Lord. The voice of the devil. The voice of someone who may be talking to you. Each voice has to be listened to and then you must decide whether you believe it or not. If someone tells you they love you, you either receive it or reject it. This is the world we live in on planet earth. Many of the words spoken hit our soul and because what Lilly would say looks like a black negative seed. They will stay in your soul until they are made to leave by replacing them with a truth. Lilly has seen them pop out while praying for healing. Lilly says they are the fiery darts that the devil throws at us and we all have gotten hit with them. Healing makes them leave and they are replaced with truth from the Lord. Let's move on here so we can actually get to the part of this story where Lilly steps into this spiritual realm.

Lilly finds herself falling in love with this musician and at this point, he is all she really has except for a few church members who loved her enough and were spiritual enough to stay with her. Lilly finds out that not only is this musician gifted with music he also knows the bible very well. Lilly was thrilled because she could never be with someone who was not on her spiritual level and this man was actually very knowledgeable in the word and was skilled at teaching and learning. He found out things from the word that Lilly was very moved by. He was very anointed. He was a very peaceful man too. Lilly needed peace. They were connecting on a spiritual level and Lilly was truly getting moved by this man. They had so much in common it was almost unbelievable. They grew up very similar and both loved the Lord. Lilly would go home by here self and pray to God about her feelings. She would know it was the Lord who put them together but why did it have to come with such a great price. She lost everybody that was dear to her. She believed God would restore her family one day. He would have to because it was the devil who tore it apart. That was the frustration of Lilly because nobody else realized it was all motivated by evil. It was to stop Lilly from ever finishing her mission of this vision. Only a man chosen by God could ever walk into the church and be perfect for the pastor's wife who died and would have the vision revealed to him too. There was no question about it. God had ordained this to be. The musician was engaged by the way only a few months before he came into the church and it all fell apart for him. That was God stopping a marriage that was not meant to be. The musician had never been married before and was kept in what he calls a prison of life. He was only released when it was his time to step in and complete the mission with Lilly. He was being set aside just for Lilly to be her husband and to both complete their final work before the second coming of the Lord. He was called some thirty years before too by God with an almost audible voice that said, " I need you now, the world is coming to an end." He says it changed his life and he got the numbers 666 and did not know what they meant but found out very quickly it was the symbol for the anti-Christ.

God was putting together a team of believers who would be compatible for marriage and ministry just like Lilly has with her late husband. He even sang like her late husband did. Lilly now sang and played the organ while the musician sang and played the guitar. They both loved it and ended up making a music CD with songs they both received from the Holy Spirit. They stood in the church and point blank asked God if they were to marry and when the prayer was said they both fell under the power of God. Lilly had to be obedient and the date was shown to them by the Lord too. Lilly did not want to get married so quickly because she knew how hurt everyone was already and this would really freak them out when they were already afraid Lilly was throwing her life away with this man. There was also only one solution to the finances and that was to marry the musician and get new daycare children. The family really had no idea how anointed she really was and how God had shined His favor on Lilly for allowing Him, without resistance, to complete His will for her life. Lilly was moving into an even greater awareness of the spirit world as her eyes opened up even more. You know what is amazing about this relationship that God put together? It had a supernatural power from the very beginning of healing. Lilly still had this cancer when she started talking to the musician and was so sick she could not eat. After she began to have true feelings of love she was able to eat again. That was before she had the operation and even knew she had cancer. The healing power of love is extraordinary. If the tumor was still there then how was it she could now eat. I say she was beginning to be healed. The musician had brokenness in his soul from this woman walking out of his life and he began to come out of his shell too. Healing began in both their lives as God had plans for them and needed them whole.

While the family suffered in their anger and fear Lilly and the musician were getting married. Lilly felt her life was not real. She continued to receive phone calls from a man who had demons influencing his life. He tried to tell her not to make this move because the whole family was against it and that Lilly was going to personally fall apart. This frightened Lilly because all she wanted to do was be obedient to the Lord. Regardless of what they all said, that she was selfish, Lilly only followed the leading of what she believed was God. This man had an agenda to take over the church and Lilly was his way in. Lilly knew from the start that this man was trouble because he was one of the people that when she met him the Holy Spirit told her to watch out for him. Lilly

133

stopped talking to him because she knew it was all demonic fear trying to keep her from the will of the Lord. This was such a disturbing time for Lilly. Other men were coming to visit in hopes of developing a relationship but Lilly couldn't separate herself from the musician. There was something about him that really moved her soul. She knew it was love. It scared her because she did not know where he was coming from in the beginning of this relationship and did not want to be acting like she was desperate for his attention but she was. She realized that she was calling him all the time and no response from him so one day she prayed about it. She had seen the women in the church chase after him when he first came and she was not going to be like them. Lilly backed off and cried all day. She said to herself, "if he is interested in me he will respond." She was not going to continue to push the issue. Her soul knew he was the one but her heart did not want to be some pushy desperate female. When he came to music practice that night he asked her why she did not call him. Lilly point blank told him that she was not chasing him and if he was not interested that was fine but she was not looking to be like the other women who tried to make a relationship and he had no interest. Lilly then walked away. That was when the musician realized he was falling for her too. It really is a beautiful love story if it had not been for the children and their anger. Lilly could not live without him. She fell head over heels in love and was stunned that she had actually found true love twice in her life. That in itself was a blessing from her God. She was so thankful for this love and for being alive. She was still broken hearted by the children but did her best to be happy. She actually was happy but was very insecure and they both had some issues to work out. His hurt from women created some issues in the marriage and her feeling insecure and needing attention also had to be healed.

They picked the wedding day because the Lord showed them the day they were supposed to be married. They only had a few people coming to the wedding because he had no family and Lilly had a family but at this time she had no family either. They were getting married in the church. The day of the wedding a hurricane was predicted to hit. Lilly did not get upset she actually was in awe over it because when she married David there also was a hurricane that disrupted the day. Lilly had a dream a week before

134

that wedding where the Lord showed her what was important were the vows taken before the Lord so she went through that wedding rejoicing too. Here she is again getting married to another love in her life and another hurricane hits. The first hurricane was Gloria and it hit a day or so before the wedding. There was no electricity so they got married by candlelight. This one was Irene and it hit the day of the wedding. Lilly laughed and looked up to God and actually thanked Him for making it a day to remember and they say rain means blessing so I guess a hurricane means the total hand of God upon it. Lilly could not believe it and took it truly as a sign from heaven that He was showering down His blessings in spite of the family rejecting her. Lilly was not going to just live with him so the choice was marriage. They had to keep this property that God intended to do something with. They moved from the church building into the house for church too. The building was in a flood zone and they both knew in their hearts that God had chosen this land for a purpose.

Before moving from the building several words from the Lord were given. A few healings took place too. Both she and the musician now miss going to the building. It was their place of peace and now it was going to be in their home. Lilly saw a demon that needed to be cast off of her future husband at the time. It was a smoking demon. She saw herself pray over him in a vision and he went to the floor by the power of God. Lilly was told not to say a word to him so as to catch the spirit unaware. That night when they both met at the church Lilly said she needed to pray for him. He agreed and when she began to pray he got very agitated and walked out of the church. Lilly got a bit nervous because she knew it was a demon. She followed after him and told him to come back inside so she could finish praying. He finally came back when he realized himself that it was the influence of the devil and one of his imps. Lilly prayed again and told the spirit to leave. He fell to the floor by the power of God and was set free. Shortly after that, he stopped smoking.

Lilly had a kidney stone that was blasted by God and disappeared. Lilly had a word from her future husband that she was going to see into the spiritual realm seven times greater than she was at this point in time and I have to say it came to pass. You will see as we move forward. The musician was ordained in the church building right after the pastor died. Lilly was told by her late husband that they intended to ordain the musician so Lilly made him the head pastor of the church being submissive to her calling as his future wife.

Jesus walked in one day while Lilly was preaching. She was standing behind the pulpit and Lilly hears the Holy Spirit tell her that Jesus is going to walk in. She heard it but was not sure what it meant. They all heard the back door slam shut really loud and nobody walked in. A few people feel something swish by them and then a woman yells out Jesus is here as she falls to her knees. Lilly then remembers what the Spirit said to her. Her son was still there at this time and he sees Jesus too. He saw the Lord with His heart of fire. It was most amazing.

Everybody watched a demon manifest itself one day as a woman fell out of her wheelchair and went into an epileptic fit. It all happened because one man decided to pray over her and he was out of the order of the Lord. The demon flung her to the floor and even though everybody prayed the ambulance had to be called. The demons then tried to jump on him because he was not under the anointing when he did it. Do not mess with the supernatural realm unless you have the power of The Holy Spirit. He did it in his flesh so he could look important. It was the same person who tried to convince Lilly she should not marry the musician. Lilly has seen some amazing things over the years. Just as The Holy Spirit moved Lilly one day to pray for a man who was an alcoholic but he jumped up and ran to leave the church. Lilly knew she was supposed to pray for him but the demon must have sensed what was going to happen because he ran. Lilly said, "where are you going?" but he just kept on going, right out the door. Unless a person is ready to be delivered they will not. Angels and demons are all around us. The demons we have to keep away from us through prayer and following the Lord. The angels we welcome for all the inspiration we can get.

7. Her Eyes Have Opened

Lilly and her now husband, the musician, have brought the church to the house where they live and the property that God miraculously provided after the flood of 2006. The property and the house were given by God. There was no income check and before the closing, the mortgage broker tells Lilly that she does not have to pay him for his services because if she did she would not have been able to get the house. He did not even know Lilly but got moved by God to tell her she did not have to pay him so they could get the house. He told Lilly that God wanted her to have this house. Lilly cried once again as she saw the hand of God step into the situation. Lilly's mom died and that was where the money came from to buy it. They had just enough money without having to pay the extra for the broker. In his kindness, he agreed not to take a fee. Who does that these days? God can influence and he did in this situation because this house is the beginning of the vision. Nobody knew it at that time. The house was signed over to the church after the Lord spoke to Lilly and told her after her husband died, that He needed it in His name which would be the not for profit ministry they started called King of Glory Ministries. Lilly obeyed. Now she lives in the house with the musician and things begin to escalate in the spiritual realm just like was prophesied over her. The prophecy that she would begin to see into this realm seven times greater.

Lilly started to see the demons clearly. Not just the demons, the angels too. She began to know where they were and what they were doing. It seemed almost unbelievable to Lilly herself but there was proof of it. When she would see a demon and notice what it was doing the person would do the very same thing she saw the demon doing. This made her look in awe at this spiritual realm. These were real beings manifesting themselves through people created in the image and likeness of God. It repulsed Lilly to know that they did this to God's creation. She would see them and rebuke them and they would go.

One person always talked about acting like a clown. She had this obsession about being a clown and would act out by moving her arms all around. The day Lilly cast this demon out she noticed it was flinging its arms all around acting goofy and the musician said to Lilly," isn't that what you told me she was doing at the church when she said she wanted to do a clown act. Lilly almost fainted because he was so right and Lilly had not thought about it until he said it. It was proof that what she was seeing was real. Creepy but they are real.

Another person who was very timid and just would follow what they were told to do was delivered. Lilly told the insecure demon to leave and she noticed it stopped at the window before leaving. She looked at it and it said to her, "what do you want me to do?" Lilly was shocked and wondered why it was asking her. It only followed orders and she was the one commanding it to leave so it was waiting to be told where to go. "Unbelievable!" Lilly thought. She had no idea. That was just how this person acted, just like the demon. Lilly told it to go to the dry places and it shot out through the window. Another woman had a demon that Lilly could see on her back. Lilly began to pray and in the spiritual realm, she grabbed the demon with her hand not touching the woman's body at all. As Lilly was pulling the demon the woman began to slide exactly the way Lilly was pulling the demon. The woman had her eyes closed and had no idea that Lilly was pulling off this being but she moved as far as the demon pulled her until it came off and Lilly threw it away to the dry places or wherever the Lord makes them go. The minute Lilly finished taking this demon off of her body and threw it, the woman stopped immediately from sliding to the right, as was the direction Lilly was pulling the demon. Sounds crazy but there was no way this woman would have done that because she didn't even know that Lilly was pulling it. This was a spiritual thing that was going on as the demon felt the power of the Spirit through Lilly's hands and it had to let go of the woman. The impy thing was embedded into her back where she was having physical pain. They do not always leave willingly so this one was holding on for dear life and actually was moving the woman sideways as it was being pulled off of her body. Lilly was in awe at all of this. She couldn't believe her own eyes. Before Lilly would pray for anyone she always made sure she was actually aware of these spirits and not just thinking them in her own mind. Lilly was getting such a keen sense in the Spirit that she began to just know that what she was sensing was real.

Driving through town one day Lilly saw a man walking humped over and she could see a demon actually morphed into his head from the hump part right into his head. In other words, the demon had molded itself to this person's body where it was disfiguring it. The person had no clue that it had a demon but Lilly knew this man had mental problems and the demon had merged into his head where it was acting out its personality of mental illness. You may think this is all crazy but these beings are real. Remember these beings are in the spiritual realm so the only way we can actually feel them is if they cause something to happen in the natural realm. We can feel their feelings when they merge with us. God's angels influence us but do not invade our free will or privacy like these evil beings do. They invade our lives and that is why they get cast out when they are revealed. Jesus rebuked demons so we are supposed to do the same thing. Not too many people want to even think about them so they remain and torment us. Lilly was so amazed by all this and wherever she went the demons knew she was able to see them. They were constantly looking at her and it made Lilly remember when she was a little girl and people were always looking at her. This time, she could see why. They knew she had the gift of discerning of spirits so they would just be curious and also concerned that she would cast them out.

Lilly watched a man walk into a store and only saw the back of him. She looked over to her husband and told him she could see a demon on his back right by his head. She could see its face and it looked at her. When the man came back out of the store he walked purposely away from her car for fear of what she might do. Lilly was so shocked because when she saw the face of the man, it looked like the demon's face. Lilly was confused about it and the only explanation she could think of was that the demon changed to be just like the man it was oppressing. That was really weird she thought. The proof was that she saw the face of the demon before she saw the face of the man and they looked the same. There was no way Lilly could have known this unless it were real.

Lilly and the musician had to go to a training class for daycare one day and when they arrived her husband said he felt the area was oppressed. Lilly said she felt it too. When they pulled

139

up Lilly could see there were demons sitting on the top of the roofs of the building. She was amazed when she could hear them talking amongst themselves and they were saying, "look at those two people, they are God's anointed." They had recognized the anointing of the Lord on them. Wow! Just like they did with Paul in the bible. It was so oppressive in that area that Lilly and the musician left and went home and never took the training that day.

When the musician and Lilly were practicing music Lilly invited the angels to come and play with them. Right after she did that she could see the room filled with angels who were playing along with them. Lilly was thrilled to see this and felt really part of the Kingdom of God. Tell me why shouldn't we be able to communicate with them if they too are in the Kingdom of our God. Enoch talked with them so why wouldn't God pick people in these end times to do the same thing. It is going to be as it was in the days of Noah so everything that was going on then will be happening now. This realm is very real and we really need those who are anointed to see them so we can stay safe. We also need the angelic protection too. Lilly found out the day the angels were all around praising the Lord with them, that special angels are assigned to ministries too. We each have a guardian angel but ministries have a guardian angel just to watch over and help keep it safe. She met this angel that day and spoke to him and his name is Petros. She speaks to them and knows what they say. What amazed Lilly was the way they talk. It really is neither male nor female. They are a combination of both but they look like men. Petros was a soft-spoken quite tall angel who danced with Lilly many nights while she was praising the Lord and listening to music. A few times the power of God was so strong that Lilly when she got too close almost fell down under the power of the Lord. I know this sounds crazy but I assure you it is not. Lilly is for real. The non-gender was what really impressed Lilly. She could just tell that Petros was not like a man or like a woman but was really both combined and it quite amazed Lilly. The way she could see this was by the way he spoke to her. He was soft spoken and gentle like a woman but had power and was authoritative like a man would be. When she would dance with the angel she would see the angel swirl around ever so beautifully like a woman would do. The power coming from this angel was very strong. It's time to

140

share a few more unbelievable things that happened to Lilly. Maybe the angel thing is a bit too much to accept for some of you but what Lilly saw happen while she was praying is undeniable.

There was a day when Lilly went out to pray in the back yard. She was speaking to the Lord and The Holy Spirit came upon her and she began to sense that the evil one was behind her watching. She did not know if it was the devil himself or an evil spirit but she felt its presence. She lifted her hands up in the air and said in a loud authoritative voice," satan get out of here in the name of Jesus." With those words being spoken immediately an extremely large tree branch came crashing to the ground right behind her and she jumped from the loud crashing sound of the branch. She thought to herself, "Oh! My God, the devil freaked out and ripped the branch off the tree in anger." She couldn't believe it. It was the power of God coming against the evil one and he reacted in a rage. Who is this emerald-eyed lady who lifts her hands in the name of Jesus and tree branches fall to the ground because spirits freak out? You think she talks to angels? I think she does. This is not all that has happened with her. Keep reading, it gets more and more intense as she walks into this spiritual realm.

That was the first encounter with the devil and rebuking him. The next encounter was during church service and Lilly had preached and was once again sensing evil lurking on the outskirts of the property. Lilly flings her arms up again while everyone watches and rebukes the devil and tells him to get lost and to stop watching them. They leave once service is over to find the tree at the corner, right next to their property, had the side branch ripped off. It was a huge branch that you could see was ripped off the side. They passed this tree going into the service and it was fine. After the rebuke, it was on the ground. No wind, no rain and nobody around either. They all looked at each other and Lilly said, "it happened when the devil was rebuked just like the other time." She was thinking to herself, "wow!" What is up with these branches being ripped off of the trees when she prays? The power of God was obviously with her.

There is the whole issue of life and death with Lilly too. People go home when she prays and people come back to life when she prays and babies are conceived when she prays. This has been happening since she was a child but it becomes more obvious as Lilly does ministry work. Lilly has a dream. In the dream, she is shown that she has to go this woman to talk to her so she can go home to be with the Lord. The musician did not want Lilly to get involved because they had left the church and there were issues going on that he did not want to get involved in. Lilly told him about the dream and she felt The Spirit wanted her to go. He told her no and she just gave it to The Lord. That night her husband had a dream and was told that Lilly was supposed to go. Lilly goes the next day to see the woman and The Holy Spirit moves her to tell the woman she was about to be with Jesus and get excited about it. You will be able to walk again on the streets of gold with Jesus she told her. The woman could no longer talk but made a sound letting Lilly know she was excited and Lilly said, "yes sister I hear you and I know you are ready to go. The Lord will take care of your children so do not worry about them." The family looked at Lilly in shock. Lilly left and the woman went home within minutes of her visit.

Another woman was suffering and Lilly lifted up her hands and said, "Father it's time for her to go home, she is in pain." Lilly was not even near the woman when she prayed that prayer, she was at her own home, but the woman died right after the prayer. It's the mercy of the Lord. Lilly is chosen for sure but she is very humble about it. She feels that many people will just not believe it and she knows it is all true. It is hard to swallow some of these amazing things that happened through Lilly but once again I assure you they are real.

I have been instructed at this point in time to stop here and explain a few things before continuing this emerald-eyed beauties story. There was a man who lived a long time ago back in the days before Noah. He is mentioned in the book of Jude in the bible when Jude refers to the book of Enoch. Enoch wrote a book just like the other disciples and prophets but what he wrote totally freaked out the human race so I believe his book was put to the side. The reason it freaked people out was because Enoch had the ability to communicate with the angelic realm. He had the ability to speak with the evil spirits too. Nobody really wants to deal with the demonic realm because it is just too disturbing for the average person to deal with. Jesus himself spoke with the angels and spoke

142

to the demons. If we are filled with The Holy Spirit, we too can and do communicate with these beings just like they did. Lilly is very concerned at this point that people just will not believe her story and had instructed me to stop and explain some of what Enoch discovered while speaking to these beings. He wrote it all down so we would know what happened to mankind just before the flood. In these days before the second coming of the Lord these truths are being revealed because the devil is launching his final attack on mankind and if the children of God do not understand or are afraid of these entities they will not know what to do when they come and try to squelch the Spirit of the living God by oppressing the children of God. You think that is not possible? Back in the day of Enoch the angels picked women and had sex with them and giants were born creating human angels. Yes, human angels with abilities. The story of the gods having sex with women and creating the Hercules of the day is not so off. I believe it comes from the truth that the angels, which were like God's to the people, sinned a great sin. In the book of Enoch in chapter 7 it goes into the whole story of how the angels began to examine the women and feel love for them. The command was given to take them and have sex to reproduce and have children. It tells that the angels were not comfortable doing this because they knew God would not approve of it. Their leader whose name was samyaza told them that if they did not follow those orders he would be punished for it. In other words, the order must have come from satan himself to do this deed. Think about it for a minute. The devil has wanted to be God and he mimics all the gifts of God so why wouldn't he take a crack at reproducing a being similar to himself. He was looking to create a race of superhumans who would be part of his army. The plan of satan is to wipe out anything that is made in the image and likeness of God. The word likeness is the key. Anyone of us who walk in the holiness of the Lord are threats to his existence. There has been a battle going on since the beginning on planet earth and most of mankind has no a clue about it. Lilly happens to be one of the children of God who have the gift to see into this realm. It really is vital in these end times because if the devil's looking to snuff out the children of God on planet earth, we have to know where and when he is going to attack. We need all the weapons that God has given us and the whole armor of God must be put on. The book of Enoch shows that these angelic beings have actual names just like we do. Each of you, who have a guardian angel, your angel has a name given to them by God. Lilly found out her angel's name is Marcos. How did she find that out? He told her. The purpose of this story is not to make Lilly out to be this amazing person, although she has been chosen by God, to do these things and see these things, but to show the children of God that we are able to walk with this supernatural power and will do what is necessary to fulfill the mission we are all called to do. Lilly has her purpose and you have your purpose. It is time for the children of God to step into this spiritual realm with the Holy Spirit and realize the supernatural is the natural with the chosen children of the Lord. Lilly feels a bit more secure with continuing her story. She hopes that you are getting it because the devil is gathering his army. His army right now has to be called by its name and its name is ISIS. ISIS means Islamic State of Iraq and Syria and the name ISIS is the name of a goddess who has been around for a long time. She is false religion and is the sorceress in the bible in Revelation. The anti-Christ will come from the Ottoman Empire which is Turkey and will fulfill his purpose before Jesus and His chosen army comes back and sends him and his army into hell. This leads to a dream that Lilly had and the musician had.

Lilly had a dream many years ago way before the world was like this. I guess you could say at least twenty years ago. She did not have the knowledge she has now and recently the reality of this dream hit her. She realized the dream was happening now. The musician had almost the same dream a few years ago and they both had these dreams before they ever knew each other existed. Very prophetic and very upsetting, but true and the body of Christ must see what the enemy once again is trying to do. Before I share the dream I have to say this. The devil is trying to wipe out all Christians. Why? He knows that Jesus is coming back to wage war against him and his demonic followers. He knows that Jesus has His army of angels and His army of human beings who have been chosen by God to be warriors for the Lord. All the Christian songs where we sing we are the army of the Lord are not just some nice words. They are fact and absolute truth. God the Father is building up His army and simultaneously the devil is doing the same thing.

The more Christians wiped out, the less army the Lord has on earth to free those who are in bondage to evil. Whatever way the devil can keep us down he will. The evil spirits that are roaming around the earth have a mission to stop whatever Christians they can from finishing their purpose. If you remember in the beginning of this story about this emerald-eyed beauty, we call Lilly, how the devil from the start had a plan to stop her. He has not succeeded but he will keep trying until Lilly becomes so full of the Holy Spirit that He can no longer find a way into her soul to bruise her. The Spirit of God has come to lead us into all truth and that truth would set us free. It is the truth that sets us free. If I pray in the name of Jesus for a person to be healed and they do not believe it, they can get healed because of the person praying's faith but when they walk away many times it comes right back. Each of us has to stand our own ground in this war. We are there for each other to lift one another up but the bottom line is we all have to have our own oil in our lamps. The truth is vital and although Lilly hates to bring attention to herself she must have people look and see where her power comes from and that we all need this same power and fire from God in the person, THE HOLY SPIRIT! Lilly hates attention especially when it is controversial but she was instructed by God to tell her story. It is time for Lilly to come out and shine the glory of the Lord to all her fellow brothers and sisters and show them it is all real. Let me remind you once again. This is a true story and now it is time to hear about the dreams the Spirit of God revealed to them both.

Lilly was walking towards a group of people in this prophetic dream. They were all sitting on the ground listening to a woman. Lilly looked at the woman and she was dressed in a gown that looked like a sorceress would look. The gown was long and flowing and she had all sorts of jewelry on her and she was throwing gifts to the people who were smiling and feeling good about what she was saying. Immediately in this dream, Lilly knew she was evil and was deceiving the people with her charm and supernatural power. They were mesmerized by her powers and truly believed she was telling the truth. Lilly felt a righteous anger over her seductress way of enticing these ignorant people into believing she had the answers to life. How dare she take the children of God and lie right to them and what upset Lilly was they were actually listening to her. Lilly began to yell to the people that she was not from the Lord but they ignored what Lilly was saying. This upset Lilly even more and at that point, Lilly stepped forward to rebuke this sorceress lady. Lilly knew she had the power to come against this evil woman because she had the Holy Spirit in her. The woman with a very serious, stern, indignant look snubbed her nose at Lilly and then turned and walked towards the people continuing her mission to deceive them. Lilly felt ill but before she could even utter a word of rebuke she knew in her soul that she could not stop it. Lilly knew it was meant to happen and she was not supposed to make it stop. It was so upsetting to Lilly and she could feel the frustration within herself because they just wanted to listen to what tickled their ears. She wanted to scream as loud as she could, "do you not see that I have the truth and she is telling the lie?" They did not see the truth but were following what the sorceress woman stood for, false religion. Prosperity and riches and nothing but joy and whatever we do wrong, God just loves us, so it is alright to sin. The dream did not end there. It moved to a next part where Lilly was walking through a building that had been destroyed somehow. It had to have been an earthquake or a bomb because parts of the building still were standing but they were not intact. Lilly was with other people who believed like she did as they all could feel the oppression of what had happened and was still happening. There were demonic beings flying all around like a bunch of bats but much larger. Lilly could see they had faces and wings and they were flitting everywhere. They were very interested in Lilly and the others and kept trying to attack their minds. As they would fly towards her they would get a few feet away and just turn around and go the other way. They could not touch Lilly and the others because the power of God was on them. They were so wanting to probe their minds that they kept trying to do this and it was annoying to Lilly who was already feeling uneasy in her soul because of what had happened in this place. Lilly had no idea what really happened but she knew evil had done it and the demons were all around trying to probe her mind and the others who were looking around trying to figure out what had happened. There was just a feeling of emptiness. No sense of God anywhere and it was so sad and disturbing to Lilly. She woke up! Lilly for years had no idea what

146

the dream meant until recently when she began to see the Christians not listening to sound doctrine but what was tickling their ears. No talk of the return of the Lord and holiness. Accepting sin as people just can't help themselves and God loves us just the way we are without any repentance at all. No need to walk in the Holiness of the Lord because God loves us just the way we are. God loves us but if He accepted us just the way we are He would not have had to send Jesus. God cannot accept the sin part of us and that is where Jesus comes in so we can receive forgiveness and repent and follow Him. It is a whole new way of life and wide is the road to destruction and narrow is the road to salvation. Few find it. That is scary but it is in the word. Lilly again wants you all to know she grieves for souls to get saved and she wants to scream as loud as she can for anyone to listen to what the SPIRIT is saying to the churches. The musician had the same basic dream but in his dream, she was throwing money to the people.

The world has come to the point where sin is being accepted as a way to live and it is alright. The bible is just some old religion that has to catch up to the times. Society has become cold hearted and does not want to hear that Jesus is the only way in. We as the children of God are becoming so irritating to the world that the devil is going to try to silence us. We must walk in the truth and the power of the Spirit or we will fall apart when things get really hard during the tribulation. Lilly walks in this realm of the Spirit and truly feels she is in this world but not part of it.

I do not want to leave out anything about the world that Lilly lives in because every detail of her life has been ordained by the God of this universe and when the bible tells us our steps are divinely ordered it sure does mean that. Whether good things or bad things happen to us every single thing we go through is perfecting us into the image of Jesus. We can complain all we want but it will not change a thing that God is trying to teach each and every one of us. We need to learn because it is vital. The army needs to listen to the officer in charge so it can win the war. Who is the officer in charge? There are three of them. The Father, the Son, and the Holy Ghost. We are predestined to be conformed to the image of Jesus the word tells us. Why? Because we are His bride and we are part of the army who will ultimately remove evil from this planet earth, which we call home. Back to the story of Lilly.

When Lilly lost her husband after being married for twenty-six years and lost her family because of it, it was very difficult for her emotionally. She loved the musician very much but her life just did not seem right. Her son was so heavy on her heart all the time because he had never been away from her and he basically got thrown into the harsh cruel world after living with both of his parents who loved him dearly. Lilly asked the Lord why it happened and she believed He told her that her son had to mature quickly because timewise things were winding down for the final finale of this world. For those who had a whole lifetime before the final tribulation, they could learn more slowly but timing is critical so things are rapidly speeding up. The exact words Lilly had heard from her husband who went home to be with the Lord. This generation whose worldly lives are going to be cut short, for the children of God, they would have to learn a few things quickly before this world as we know it changes for the worst. Lilly, although she was heartbroken, knew God always had a plan even when evil stepped in. Waiting was the hardest thing for Lilly. Her son had left in anger and went through his own hell as he matured. Lilly had nobody but the musician and a few church members who did not walk away too. Lilly was moving in this spiritual realm with unbelievable accuracy and was watching this realm participate in their everyday lives as they had angels watching over the land behind the house for the future Christian community to be built. Lilly could see these angels and then she read about other places who were intending to build such places too. She began to watch a show with a known pastor who was already building a place for the children of God to live during these end times. She was learning about Revelation and what was going to come down the pike so to speak. As scary as it seemed she was excited in her soul to know that Jesus was coming back sooner than she had thought. She just might be alive when all this happens. Storing food for this time to come was her goal. Becoming self-sufficient was also the goal. It was amazing to her how everything was falling into place in the world according to the book of Revelation. These safe havens were being built and there were certain areas, that were told to preachers, years ago that were the areas that God would have His angels protecting. Lilly lived in one of these areas and was amazed because she moved up to this area years ago not even knowing that God was sending her here for this very purpose. With no money to buy this land Lilly just kept believing God would do whatever was necessary to make it happen. Lilly had seen enough miracles to know that God had no problem. The problem was Lilly and her patience in waiting. This reminds me of the time when Lilly was very poor and she had put fifty dollars in the drawer so she could buy Christmas presents for her children. Lilly was separated from her husband back then and when a Christian brother needed fifty dollars, so his mother's electricity would not get cut off, Lilly felt the tugging of the Spirit to give him the money she had for her children's Christmas. It was a hard decision but Lilly knew that God would take care of her children for Christmas and He did. Lilly felt so happy when the brother cried and thanked her because he did not have the means to help his mom that day. Lilly had the exact amount of money needed that day to help and she obeyed the leading of the Spirit. Another time Lilly had food put away for the week and had no money to buy any more food. A person called for food and Lilly took half of what she had and gave it to them cutting her own food supply. What happened next was God stepping into the picture. A brother in the Lord came to the house and told her that God had told him to buy Chinese food for dinner that night. He brought the food and he also brought desert. He came for the rest of the week with all the food each day she needed for her and her two children. Lilly was so thrilled to see that God had truly stepped in to help her just because she took from her lack to help someone else in need. These were real lessons learned of how our Father's Kingdom works. Had to tell these because it is all part of Lilly's life and the wonderful God she serves.

Back to this part of her life where they were having church at the house that the Lord had given them by a miracle. After her husband died and Lilly had married the musician, one of the women in the church had heart problems and lung problems. She was not really taking care of herself the way she should have been and had to be rushed to the hospital. Lilly was called for prayer.

Lilly knew she was having the same problem her late husband had with his heart and the lungs and she all of a sudden got a knowing that she was going to die. Lilly cried out to her Father God and asked Him not to take her home yet. She pleaded with Him to have mercy on her because she could not bear to lose another person she loved at this time. Her whole family was out of her life and this woman was one of the few who loved her and understood what God had done between her and the musician. Lilly said these words with tears running down her face, "please God do not take her home yet. I need her here with me. Please let it not be the time for her to go!" She felt a connection with the Father at that moment and she knew He was going to save her life. What was happening in the hospital while this prayer from Lilly was being said was all of a sudden the woman died. The spirit of death, this was one that sucks the breath out of a person's lungs, he was attacking her. It had made its attack when she was home. What it did may frighten some of you but this is all part of this life. We just do not see it going on unless we are aware of it. The demons are used by God too, so we do not have to fear them. Remember the bible does tell us that all things do work together for good for those who love the Lord. This woman truly loved the Lord. She was not perfect and should have been taking care of herself better than she was but God is very merciful and He listened to Lilly's heart as she shared her feelings with Him. The demon who was sent by the devil to kill her was sitting on her couch waiting for the right moment in time to do the dirty deed. He was so excited he could hardly contain himself while he waited for the signal to make his move. Lilly's friend was very depressed that day and this was a form of weakness that gives humans a vulnerable opening for these impy things to attack. The woman was supposed to be doing breathing treatments but because she was so down about her life she missed the treatments for weeks and the lungs were weak. All of these factors played a role in this moment of time when harlo, which was his name, flew across the room and sat on her shoulder. That day her dog kept barking and she could not understand why. It saw the demon and was reacting to it. The nasty little thing shoved his fist into her nostrils to keep the air flow from coming in. The woman then opened her mouth to breath. Another imp came from roaming about seeking whom

150

he may devour and put pressure on her lungs. The two of them were squeezing the life out of her. A third spirit flew in through the window and told her she was going to die and panic mode set in. Her heart began to stress out from the lack of oxygen and the panic feeling she had. Time to go to the emergency room. They were all laughing so loud it's a no wonder everybody didn't hear them. To them, it was a game and a trophy to win when death would come and the life was snuffed away. Thank God we have Jesus and the Father and The Holy Spirit. We truly must understand who our strength comes from and how we have the power in Jesus' name. While the demons were having their sick fun and games Lilly was diligently praying for her not to die. She did die from the attack. She was told after she came back that she had died but then just started to breathe again. It was at the same time Lilly was asking her Father in heaven to save her life because she got a knowing what was about to happen. You cannot say these are just coincidences. These are actual prayers being heard by God and being answered. Again the anointing that Lilly has was being used. When Lilly heard what had happened she looked up to heaven and cried with thanksgiving at the mercy of her God on her soul, that was still so broken by the trauma she had been through, of losing her husband to death.

Time moves on and Lilly has episodes where she talks to the angels and knows what they are saying to her. She is praying one day and she hears the angel Petros, who is the ministry angel, tell her she needs to call one of the women who left the church. He said she was not in a very good place and needed help. When Lilly makes the phone call, sure enough, she is ready to go to the mental hospital. Lilly prays for her and she settles down. Another time she and the musician were driving down the hill and Lilly hears her angel, Marcos, tell her that they need to slow down there is going to be a deer crossing the road in front of them. She tells her husband and he slows up. Sure enough, the deer comes out and they were spared a possible hit. You cannot say that Lilly does not hear them because it proves itself out. As crazy as it sounds this supernatural realm is more real than we are. We will pass away from this physical realm into the spiritual realm for eternity so what realm is actually the everlasting realm? What realm will be real to us when we die or go in the rapture and have new bodies that are indestructible? How real is that? How did Jesus walk on the water? He was flesh was He not? He walked on the water in a flesh body. This leads me to another thing that happened to Lilly some years ago with her late husband. As I am writing about her life things come to me. I do not want to leave out these amazing situations because they are just too interesting and supernatural to ignore.

Lilly and her husband at the time had to travel a distance to bring a person home. The trip was about an hour and a half. They had to take this person back so it was a necessary trip to be made. They had a church service that night and had to be back. To make a long story short the timing was not falling into place the way it needed to be and there was going to be no way to get back in time for the service. They had underestimated the distance they had to go to bring this person home and now they were surely going to be late. Lilly was freaking out because one thing she hated and that was to be late for anything. She always had time pressure on her from being in school and having to finish within time limits and she just hated when she knew she had to get somewhere at a certain time. She always made sure she had plenty of time to be somewhere so this was creating stress for her. She knew it was inevitable that they were going to be late. It took so many minutes to get there and the same route back would be about the same time. Maybe a few minutes less depending on how fast they went but they were going to be at least twenty to thirty minutes late. She felt terrible because there would be people waiting there for them and wondering where they were. As they were driving they started to talk about the Lord and how great He was. Lilly took her mind off of the time. She hears her husband say, "there's the turn-off." Lilly looked at the time and saw that they went from one point to this point with hardly any time change. They looked at each other with surprise and knew something weird had happened. Time seemed to stop or they got transported to the exit. There was no other explanation for what had happened. They not only got there, they were early. No explanation to this day! When the rapture takes place our bodies will be changed in the twinkling of an eye the word tells us. That is how quick God can change whatever He wants to. Who is to say He would not make a car and two people in the twinkling of an eye be where

152

they needed to be. He did it in the word with His people back in the day so why not today. He is the same yesterday, today and forever!

They drove a couple to the airport to make a flight for a trip the couple was making to an orphanage they had built overseas. They were not sure what exist they had to get off. All of a sudden the four of them including Lilly heard a voice that spoke with authority say," turn to the right." Her husband instinctively turned figuring it was a police officer but there was nobody behind him. It was the exact exit they had to turn off on to get to the airport on time. They just made it. If it were not for the voice telling them to turn to the right they would have missed the exit and the flight. It was an audible voice that they all heard and not one of them had said it. Who was the voice that saved the day?

While I am telling these stories of Lilly's life I have a heartbreaker that will make you see the torment some people actually go through in this life when evil spirits latch onto them and constantly speak words of fear. Her name has been changed but we will call her Sarah. Sarah met Lilly at a well-known Christian organization where Lilly worked as a phone counselor. I mention the dream Lilly had about this woman in the beginning of the story but I feel the need to tell the whole thing. Lilly has this dream about a woman coming into the club and she had demons that needed to be cast out. Lilly had never done this before but the dream was so real she kind of knew what to do. This woman walks in and looks about as creepy as one can get. She was bowed over and her hands were out to the side of her as she looked around the room. She was so fearful and it was so obvious she was being tormented by demons. Lilly watched from across the room as her head moved from side to side very methodically like a robot and everyone could tell immediately that something was not normal with her. Lilly remembered the dream she had a week before and realized it was the woman in her dream. She got a bit nervous when she realized the dream was from the Lord and they were probably going to cast out this demon or demons. Lilly got nervous in her soul because dealing with evil is not exactly what she had planned to do that day or any day for that matter. The woman asked for prayer because she knew she had these spirits so Lilly and David, who was there too, took her in a private room and began to pray for her. The evil spirit was actually seen by her older son and he described it as a gremlin looking thing, sitting on her shoulder. It would speak into her ear the words it was saying and she would repeat them.

I have to say this at this point in this book because the church is very ignorant to this part of the gospel message. They go about their everyday lives and are so unaware that these evil spirits are around all the time looking to find a person who is vulnerable. You do not have to be involved with the devil's territory to have them come on you. All you have to do is have a weakness in the flesh and if you do not walk with the Lord they will just come and join up with you. If people do not tell them to leave they will just stay and do whatever their personality is. May I say none of their personalities are good. Christians have to start realizing that before some of you walked with the Lord you had lives that were not so pleasing to God and you opened up to these spirits. Now you walk with the Lord but you have some things to clean up and you cannot understand why you keep doing the same thing wrong over and over again. It could be one of these imps that have clung onto you. Not to put fear on you, but we need to understand. All you have to do is tell them to go in the name of Jesus and they leave. They have to leave but if they came because you enjoyed a sin before getting saved they don't just fly away. They are there to stay until they are commanded to leave or the anointing is so strong they cannot take it, so they run to escape the torment they feel when the power of God hits them. They are desperate to have bodies to manipulate otherwise they just fly around with nothing to do. As creepy as that sounds it is all part of this world we live in. We must function with the entire message of our Lord not just what we want to hear. The full message brings deliverance for God's people. Anything less will keep the child of God in bondage. It is time for the church to stop being so afraid of the devil and confront him when necessary. We are not to feel humiliated by it either because these beings just wait for opportunities to attach to humans. All have fallen short in this life and Jesus came to set the captives free. He cast out many demons and so did the disciples. We should be doing the same thing to free the bride of the Lord. Before the return of Jesus, Christians will be understanding this and getting set free. These beings are an abomination to God and coming against any child of God is unacceptable to God our Father. We house the Holy Spirit and He certainly does not want anything hindering what He needs to do to lead people to the truth and convict the sinner to repentance. The fewer people these beings can latch onto, the stronger the body of Christ becomes. The purpose for the devil is to keep the Christians down in whatever way he can do it. We need to start fighting back against all manner of evil and stop denying we might have some issues to clean up. The truth is what sets us free. In these end times, truth is very much needed. The world has been following so many lies, we no longer know the difference between what is the truth and what are the lies.

Back to Sarah and her dilemma of these beings who have invaded her life. Lilly started to pray and she no sooner opened her mouth and this being started to manifest itself by screaming when Lilly said she was washed in the blood of Jesus. Lilly was stunned and the dream came right to her remembrance once again. She said for it to come out of her and it began to talk right to Lilly. She looked up at Lilly and began to talk about Lilly's personal life. Lilly was amazed at this being and got creeped out at the same time. It proceeded to say," I am going to ask my father satan to put a sleep on you people." Then it looked Lilly right in the eye and said, "I'm going to get you." Lilly felt a bit of fear and wondered what was his plan for her. Instead of focusing on the words spoken she rebuked it in the name of Jesus and Sarah began to scream some more. She told Lilly she was thirsty and could she have a drink of water. Lilly brought her back a glass of water and she took a sip and spit it back into Lilly's face. Lilly realized the demon was actually talking through Sarah and Lilly could not believe what was happening. This was like some horror picture she thought. Is this for real, she was thinking. She knew it was, she was right there experiencing it. These creatures were disgusting and how dare they do this to the image and likeness of God. She stood up and got violent and caught David off guard and knocked him and another man to the floor. None of them had any experience with demons and this sure was a lesson learned. They did not take their authority in the Lord and use it properly. demons have to be told to be quiet and not to manifest themselves. They battled way more than they needed to but after hours of this ordeal, she was somewhat free. She had a bunch of these spirits but after Lilly and David finished she was able to have a conversation with them. I'm not really sure what her problem was because she kept coming back over the years and still had issues, but she was never as bad as she was the first time she was prayed over. We don't always know the lifestyle of people either. They may be doing things to bring in these beings.

Sarah joined the church and Lilly always had her guard up because she knew she still had problems. One day in the dead of winter Sarah called and said she had nowhere to live and was in the street with her daughter. Lilly was heartbroken for her and they had a finished room in the basement, so out of love they told her she could come and stay with them until something worked out. The ex-husband came and took the daughter and got custody of her. Sarah was now living with Lilly and her family. Lilly did not trust her and when they went to sleep at night Lilly made sure there was a lock on the door so she could not come into their section of the house. It was not a very comfortable atmosphere and this was only temporary. She started doing weird things and Lilly had no idea she was this messed up. It was so upsetting to see her be so tormented. She would come up in the middle of the night and take one cookie and bite it and put it back on the tray. She would bite the cookie and then get panicked and feel guilty so she would have to put it back. She went to make popcorn one night and forgot it was on and the smoke alarm went off. Thank God for smoke detectors because she set the pan on fire. Lilly knew this was not good for her children so she started asking questions as to why she was not living with her mom anymore. There was no reason she could not just go home accept she was being rebellious and did not want to. It was time to take Sarah home where she needed to be. Lilly was a bit angry about the whole situation because she made it sound like she was not allowed to live there anymore and that was just a lie. Lilly had put herself out for her and it was affecting her family and Sarah was a liar and still had spirits. Lilly had no clue what was really wrong so she told her to get her things because she had to take her home. She began to act out and throw her things around the room. Lilly was getting angry and told her with authority to pick up her things, now. She finally did it and she was brought back home to her house. Lilly felt free and told herself she was never going to do that again. She did it out of love but maybe it was not what she was supposed to do. Live and learn! Dealing with demons and casting them out is one thing, living with one is another. The person has to want to be free or you are wasting your time. Not saying Sarah was one of those who did not want to be free but she had been prayed over many times and still was the same way. There was more involved than Lilly had an idea of. So sad and so disturbing to see such torment.

This was not the only time Lilly did this even though she said she would never take in a mentally ill person again. When she moved back upstate after watching the teenagers who had mental issues in the home she took one of them with her because she was going to end up in some home where Lilly knew she would be thrown into the system with no one to love her. She loved Lilly's son and Lilly thought things would be alright. Once again Lilly went by her feelings and never really prayed about what to do. They moved and the girl was eighteen years old now with a younger child's mind. She was able to stay by herself so Lilly had to go out and leave her alone one day. She was gone for a while and when she came back she could see she was very upset. Lilly asked if she was alright and she said she was. When Lilly went upstairs to the bathroom she saw that the girl had vomited all over the entire bathroom. Lilly was beside herself. She could not believe her eyes and realized once again where was her head at when she thought if she showed this girl love it would heal her. There was definitely more than love needed and Lilly at this time in her life knew about demons but did not have the knowledge of what to do about them. She did not want to get into casting out spirits and maybe it was just plain craziness and no spirits were even involved. She was not going to mess with it because maybe the girl would really go crazy. Lilly was too afraid to touch it. Lilly prayed for the Lord to make a way for her to leave and get the real help she needed. "Why did she do this to herself?", Lilly thought. She was learning first-hand about these beings and how disgusting they really were. In the home where this girl lived with them, they had three others with problems too. One girl used to defecate and smear it onto the walls. What manner of perversion was this? It had to be evil spirits. It was so disturbing to Lilly. The Lord made the way for her to be taken to the hospital where she could get the help she needed. There is one more part to this bizarre story before she left. This girl went to a counselor who told her if she felt frustrated she could take a rubber band and put it on her wrist and snap it. This was supposed to keep her from actually taking a knife and cutting herself with it. Now that she had permission to abuse herself with the rubber band what do you think she did? Exactly! It was a sick demon, that if Lilly had really known about, she would have rebuked it really quickly. It came and showed up for the fun of it all. This day this pervert imp jumped on the bandwagon to really have a blast tormenting this kid. It sat on her shoulder right next to her ear and started to methodically repeat, "snap your wrist and feel the burn. Enjoy the pain a lesson learned. This is the way to ignore your hurts and the more you burn the more you will feel relief. Come on now feel the pain, you know you like it. It's just what the doctor ordered so keep on snapping that rubber band and feel better." Then the demon just kept getting louder and louder with the words, "snap the rubber band, snap the rubber band." When Lilly saw what she did to her wrists she asked her why she did it and she told her what the counselor had said. Lilly was furious at the counselor for giving her permission to do this. What a sick thing to tell her to do. The counselor was very upset because her theory was to keep her from hurting herself. Lilly told her, "did you not think it would give her an excuse to just keep doing it until it was so red and sore?" After this thing escalated and she just manifested more and more bizarre behaviors so she had to be picked up by the police and brought in for help. Lilly never took her back and felt terrible that she tried to love her and it just did not work. There was more than love needed. Looking back at it now Lilly would say there was deliverance from evil spirits that was needed. Mentally ill people very rarely ever recover because who do you know that casts out devils so people can be free? Lilly hates dealing with them. She knows all about them now but to this day she despises them all. The thought of these beings motivating humans made in the image of God just makes Lilly feel disgusted. This is the world we live in and believe me it is not going to get any better until Jesus returns. We had better get a clue how to deal with these entities that are just as real as we are.

There was the witch that Lilly encountered in church service one day. She came in and sat towards the front. Lilly sensed evil and could actually feel it coming at her. She was wondering what was going on. It got so strong that Lilly had to leave the building for a bit to get rid of the pressure she was feeling. She had never had this feeling during service ever before and was not sure what was going on. She did know it was an evil force coming at her. She finally noticed the woman sitting in the seat staring at her with a look of hatred and realized it was a demon. After service was over the woman walked right up to her with anger and point blank told Lilly, "I'm a witch and I don't like you." Lilly felt the anger and said back to her, "I know, you have a spirit." Lilly walked away because she knew she did not want to be free. Lilly never saw her again.

8. Talking to an Angel

I cannot tell you how many demons Lilly has encountered in her life or I would be writing forever. You can get the point. They are out there and Lilly knows very well why they are there. Lilly was becoming more and more involved in this spiritual realm. After Lilly lost the love of her life and lost everything that was dear to her she became unattached to this life completely. If she could endure the trauma of losing the man who held her heart and was her spiritual counselor, besides the Lord, nothing else really mattered to her anymore. There was only one person in her life who God obviously had sent to help her finish the mission of the vision. The vision that her late husband had and the message that he found floating in the water. There was nobody more qualified than the musician and Lilly loved him dearly. He was so similar to her late husband it was almost scary. He said things and did things just like her husband had done. It could not have been a more perfect match. It was not the plan of Lilly for sure and the musician had his eyes on another woman when he came into the church. God took the love of Lilly's life away and God removed the woman from the musician's life too. He had never been married before and was free to marry Lilly. Nothing in the way of God's plan to build this place of refuge for His children during the tribulation which was coming on the earth. Many disagree with this but time will tell who is on the right side of the rapture and how close we really are to the end of the world, as we know it. We all agree on one thing and that is Jesus is coming back again. If things get really bad and we have to go through the entire tribulation period, the Christians had better make some preparations for it. There is nowhere in scripture that tells of a rapture before the tribulation so we better get ready for the upcoming events. They are all in the book of Revelation. The book that nobody wants to read or know about. Too scary for most but that does not mean it is not going to happen. The clouds are moving in and the storm is coming. It has begun already with what Jesus calls the beginning of birth pains. I just realized why He refers it all to birth pains. Birth pains intensify as time gets closer to the birth. So too will the events escalate and get more and more intense until the birth of the true church emerges and is born. The true church not the luke- warm church. The true bride of Jesus is the one He is coming to rescue. We cannot become His bride unless we die to self and take on the power of the Spirit and walk with Him. During this tribulation, the true Christians will get on fire and truly become His bride. It cannot happen without letting go of the flesh side of us and recognizing the Holy Spirit and walking in the spirit realm rather than the flesh. We are in this world but not of this world. That is what it means. Lilly walked into this realm already because she lost it all and her love for Jesus blossomed and nothing else truly mattered. She has a purpose and that is what she focuses on. She walks with God every day. She suffers for His name sake all the time. Demons have targeted her throughout her whole life. She lived and she learned how to recognize this other world which also needs to be recognized by all the children of God. The spiritual world is where everything functions. When we come back with Jesus for the battle of Armageddon, we will be spiritual beings and will be sending demons to hell. It is time to come into the new life with God and His angels and to recognize that we are battling with the devil and all of his army.

When Lilly's son walked out the door. It was more of an impact in this spiritual realm than anyone had any idea of. It split the very core of the ministry. It was the father, Lilly and the son who were together in this vision. This is the prophesied son who obviously has some kind of a purpose in all this end time stuff too. He is young but has been called of God. He too had a vision of Jesus coming to him and showing him His heart of fire. When he left in anger and hurt and Lilly was devastated because nobody could see what God was doing with the musician. The devil was thrilled. That day when he walked out the door Lilly was broken once again. She was torn between her son and what she knew God was doing with the musician coming into her life. Lilly tried her best to make her son understand what God was doing and that she loved his father with all of her heart. She knew from the words of her late husband that God had said the timing was very critical. That means everything needs to follow suite to God's plan. The devil himself steps up his game plan in this. He still had to bring Lilly down so another way to destroy her ability to function would be to take the second love of her life away, her son. The only son who really had anything to do with her life. Her other son had pretty much decided to condemn her for what he felt was her neglect over the years because of the poverty they had to endure. He felt she should have fixed things and did not according to his expectations. He had no relationship with her. He was not looking to God and it seemed like he walked away from believing anything. Lilly just prayed for him all the time. Her second son was a miracle of God because he was born dead and came back to life. He had some kind of a purpose for God or God would have taken him home that day when he was born dead. This was the devil's plan to keep everybody involved so upset and sad that nothing would be accomplished.

I know I have already spoken of some of this but I am winding down to the end of this story and have to make the impact of what really took place that day when her son left. Lilly had no idea the real significance of this until recently so it is important to reiterate what actually happened in the spiritual realm that day. With the loss of her husband Lilly was vulnerable to demonic attack. The family all relied on the father for their spiritual strength and he was gone. Lilly too depended on him for her spiritual strength. Nobody had the answers accept Lilly who knew what God was doing. That did not help her with her fear of being alone and what to do about money and her realizing her son was not accepting her relationship with the musician. Lilly was so torn and kept going to the Lord about what to do. She knew she was losing her son while she was gaining a friendship and falling in love. The enemy was tormenting her with this decision she was going to have to make. She would go to bed and battle with fear and feel guilty. The devil was truly attacking them all with his demons of anger and fear. He was thrilled to see it all falling apart. Now that the head of the church was gone, satan would tumble them all, like a bunch of dominoes.

He was with his crony demons and success was being celebrated as Lilly and her son grew further and further apart. They had been so close even though her son was a loner and pretty much did his own thing. There was love, and it was from heaven above with all the miracles God had done to make this a family unit of love and to have compassion for the children of God.

They had fed the needy since 1984 and helped families from getting evicted. They had given families their own beds and slept on the floor for weeks until they could get a bed for themselves. The sacrifice they made to feed the needy when they were poor themselves was their legacy. Their son had watched this and was so proud of his father. Now it was all over. Everyone thought that because the father had died the whole ministry would collapse. The devil himself was sure of it and was already celebrating in the lower chambers of his abode, wherever that is, while he waits to be thrown into the lake of fire. This was a day of trauma and destruction for the family and the beginning of a long road back to recuperation and forgiveness and understanding. Listen to what these disgusting evil beings did that day.

satan from the beginning as we know had it in for Lilly. His jealousy was so intense that her whole life he did nothing but try to hinder her walk with God. He did emotionally get to her many times over the years but God always picked her up and kept her going. She was never stopped by this evil angel. This day he called all the demons and they were having what we would call a victory party. What they did was bizarre and weird. They dug up dirt from the ground. They gathered it into a pile. Then they took human bones from some graves that were near the area. The bones were from men who had been murdered and the one who murdered them tried to hide the body by burying it. Since the demons were the ones who influenced the murder they knew exactly where to find these bones for this ritual they were about to perform. They piled these bones on top of the pile of dirt and all stood around it and began to chant some repetitious babble. satan opened his mouth and lit the whole mound of dirt and bones on fire as he laughed and contorted in a way that would make you feel ill if you watched it. The rest of the demons kept the chant going and encircled this mound of dirt and bones as if it was a treasure or a trophy they had just won. They were swinging their winged arms up and down and bending over at the same time. They would come back up again as this screeching, ear-piercing sound came from them. It was a real ritualistic expression of victory. If I tell you the words they were chanting you might get righteous anger but this is what happens in the world of the demonic and we better realize we have real enemies out there who

163

enjoy watching us suffer. They were mocking the creation of man when they kept repeating these words, "you were made from dirt and we will send you all back to the dirt. We will take you to the fire and watch you burn. There is no Savior for you. Burn, burn, burn you fools who believe. We will destroy every last one of you. Aha, Aha!"

Lilly's son walked out the door that sad day and when he left he took a box that Lilly had put all her late husband's personal things in that she wanted to keep. She had put it in her son's room but she did not realize he was going to take it with him. That day the demons spoke to her son and convinced him this was the only answer, to leave. He was not going to deal with the musician. Lilly was trying to be honest and told her son that she was meant to marry him. Anger at her son's reaction provoked the words," you can get out if you do not like it." He didn't like it and he left feeling Lilly had thrown him out. She was so emotionally drained by his anger every day at her when she knew it was not her fault and God had ordained this not her. Everyone was so drained by the emotional trauma and feelings were running crazy thanks to all the evil spirits who were so thrilled at their accomplishment. Lilly could not take it anymore. Her son just had such anger it was not even normal. It was not normal; it was an attack on him.

He walks out and Lilly breaks down and cries her heart out. It was not what she wanted, but there was no other way at this time. Because the musician was in her life and because of God, Lilly had to obey what she knew God was doing. The musician came in to help Lilly emotionally and step into the position that God ordained for him. The mission from satan was successful; total disruption of the family unit. Her son walked out the door with the miraculous message from the sea that his father had gotten from God. When Lilly realized he had taken all of her husband's personal things she was upset. This message from the sea was very important to the ministry and this was the word from the Lord of what this ministry was supposed to do. It was directly from God and Lilly did not want it to get lost or ruined.

Years earlier because of money problems they were evicted and when you get evicted they come in and throw all your belongings onto the street. It is up to you to take them or leave them. Usually, people come by and steal your things before you

164

can even have them picked up. It is quite humiliating. The day they left Lilly took one more look at the things left on the street and she saw the message from the sea in the picture frame it was in. It was sitting on top of all the things, and Lilly jumped out of the car to grab it. It would have been lost. God made Lilly find it and Lilly made sure from that day it would never get misplaced again. She did not know at that time that this message was not just a personal word for her husband but was an actual confirmation of what this ministry was meant to do. She did know it was very special to David so that was why she grabbed it. She also knew it was sent by God. Her husband never let it out of his sight, ever again either.

I am going to share a conversation Lilly had with one of the angels. We have heard enough about the demons in this story so let's listen to some angelic words spoken. Lilly really became aware of these angels and how much they really interacted with us one day while having music practice. She invited them to come and join them in their time of singing and playing before the Lord. When Lilly invited them to come she just got a knowing that they showed up. She felt joyful and told the musician, who was now married to her, that she could see these angels playing music with them. She watched others dancing around so gracefully. They were flowing as if they blended in with the music and the air around them. In other words, they were so in sync with the music and the rhythm and they were literally floating around in the air. Lilly cried as she watched these beautiful angelic beings praise the Lord with them. It was so obvious to her that they were neither male nor female, by the way, they were dancing around. Lilly was amazed and just stared at them. She could hardly play the organ as she gazed at the glory of God shining from each one. They were so opposite the demonic spirits. Peace flowed from them and Lilly realized that she had invited them and they came. This became a regular thing every time they practiced. Lilly began to connect with them. She noticed one very large angel who stood right in the center of the room. He was as tall as the ceiling and Lilly knew he was there all the time. She finally got up the nerve to ask him why he was there. She asked and when he responded she got so excited. She could not believe this was actually happening but she knew in her spirit and soul it was real. Her mind was telling her she was crazy but her spirit and soul knew it was real. The angel responded to her question with these words, "I am the angel assigned to watch over the ministry." Lilly asked him if he had a name. She was not sure what she was allowed to ask but she felt comfortable in finding out what was happening to her. The angel replied and said, "we all have names given to us by God and my name is Petros." Lilly was in awe that she was having a conversation with this angel. She just knew it was real. She walked over to where he was and asked him if he would touch her. She stood in front of him and as she sensed him touching her she felt a surge of power go through her and it almost knocked her off her feet. Her mind once again said, "this is all in your imagination." She knew it was the enemy trying to steal what was happening. Lilly knew it was real. She asked if she could put on the CD they made and dance with him together before the Lord. She had watched him dance and felt so peaceful by his angelic moves and she wanted to experience what it would feel like to dance with an angel before God. It was such an honor she felt to be able to step into this realm and be part of it. Lilly was learning that this angelic realm was very much a part of our world and it was just that we did not know it. Lilly was getting a taste of what is was to actually talk and be part of the real Kingdom of God. This was part of the Kingdom that we would have to accept and allow to be part of our lives. The angels are the ministering spirits for us. Jesus had them come and help Him and He was part of that realm right here on earth to. Why not the rest of God's children.? Time for the church to wake up and see the full Kingdom operating here on earth. Lilly was so filled with joy she could hardly contain herself. She put on the music as her husband watched this most unbelievable dance before the Lord. Lilly was overwhelmed when she began to twirl around like the angel was doing and move around in a circle with him. He was so involved in his praising of God and Lilly could see that he was truly one with the God of the universe. It taught her a thing about true oneness with God as she watched him be engulfed with love and peace. He had no interest in seeing what Lilly was doing as she danced because he was so focused on God. It was as if he was in a whole other world, for real. What a difference between them and us. We focus on everything down here and they pay no attention to anything down here except for when they are needed to help. Their total lives are existing in the presence of God. Lilly twirled around and touched Petros and fell to the ground under the power of God. She got up and laughed and enjoyed this supernatural time with the angel. It was one of the most amazing experiences she ever had and the connection to this realm became very real to her that day. She actually felt all this love for these beings that God created and almost wanted to worship them because the feeling was so uplifting that she truly felt she was not part of this world anymore and wanted to show her appreciation to them. She knew they were just like she was, a servant of the Most High God. Lilly felt a real kindred spirit with them all and was so thrilled to be part of God's Kingdom, right here and now. After that encounter, Lilly knew what the bible meant when it says that we are is in this world but not of this world. Our connection to this life is our flesh but if we operate in the spirit we will and can see into this spiritual realm. The supernatural is truly the natural to all those who believe what Jesus said and did. This is how the disciples lived their lives too. What changed from that time? Nothing did! People just strayed away from the truth over the generations and followed their own lust and desires and pushed God out. The world today has pretty much told God they do not want to follow Him and they have made up their own rules. Believing the life that Lilly lives is just too Holy and the average person will not look up and take their eyes off of themselves to find God. Even if they find God through His Son they find it hard to believe in miracles and angels that interact with us for the good and for the bad. It is just too much to take in and the interest is in having fun and enjoying everything in this life that satisfies. What people do not understand is there is nothing satisfying in this life because it comes and it goes. The world that Lilly has connected to is for eternity and when her body stops because of death, her spirit will just move out and into her spiritual body and continue with God. Is this emerald-eyed beauty so different from everyone else? It is a shame to say but I think she is because most are too self-absorbed. Lilly so desperately wants you who are reading her story to believe because it is true and also because she loves her God and wants you all to know how much He loves you too. Her husband, the musician, watches in awe as Lilly encounters these angels more and more.

Lilly was very curious one day and asked Petros about his emotions. Petros told her that he was only allowed to answer the questions that he was given permission from God to answer. Lilly understood but she was so comfortable with her God and she knew God was teaching her about this realm that not too many people were even aware of. It was the most exciting thing that was happening to Lilly and it was prophesied that she would begin to operate seven times stronger in this gift than she had before. Petros was given permission to explain to Lilly about their personalities. He said, "We have feelings too but the downfall of man is you are controlled by your feelings. We are in the very presence of God and we are controlled by the feelings of peace, joy and all the assurance that everything is alright. You have to deal with the evil in the world and all the influences that we do not have." He then told Lilly something and what he said touched her heart so much that it made her cry. He told her that they marvel at us for the love we have for God in spite of all the terrible things the devil does to us. With all that we have to endure through all the trials and tribulations of this life, they marvel that we will not give up and just keep loving God. He went on to say they are glad they are not human because of all we have to endure but how wonderful it is to be human. It was so true. Lilly knew it was a real conversation because it was so true. Lilly always aired on the side of caution because she knew how the devil could come in as an angel of light to deceive. Lilly had dealt with enough demons over the years and did not want one to be acting like one of God's angels to lead her astray. This was really the first time since she had seen the angel in the corner of her room so many years ago that she was involved with the angelic realm. Most of her ministry was dealing with demons and how creepy it was. She was so thankful for these moments in time to learn about these most beautiful beings created by God too. Technically we were all part of this same Kingdom. Why should man be so ignorant to these beings? Lilly for the first time in her life began to realize how anointed she was. She humbly realized that all the things that had happened to her over the years were because she was chosen by God and was gifted by the Holy Spirit. She was not just some

168

ordinary person. She had never met one person who had prayed for someone who was dead to come back to life and it happened. What was God doing with her? Why was she doing these amazing things? She knew it was all God but why did he pick her to do them? Lilly was just so humble it really was hard for her to grab that she was a chosen vessel of honor for the Lord. She would always say when people would be in awe over some of the things that she had seen and put her up on some kind of pedestal, "I just love the Lord and want to finish my purpose for him in this life." She has never taken any glory for herself because she always knew, even as a child, that whatever gifts or talents one has they were God given so therefore there is no need to brag unless you brag in what the Lord has done. Lilly could never understand how people thought who they were because they were good looking. They did not make themselves good looking so why would they think they were special because of it. Lilly was just thankful for any blessing God had given her. She knew she was blessed to have found true love twice in her life because some people never find it. Lilly had never taken for granted the gifts from God. Her life was a gift from God and God saved her from dying of cancer. There is another part to the story about the colon cancer that Lilly had, and I am going to tell you now another miracle given from the Most High God.

The musician and Lilly decided to go see a well-known preacher who was coming about two hours away from them. They traveled to get there and they were so excited about this. The service was thrilling as all the children of God sang songs of praise. During one part of the service, the pastor was receiving words of knowledge for the people from the Lord. A word of knowledge means that he was being told by The Holy Spirit what God was going to do with certain people who were there. He would say God is healing someone of diabetes or anything else. Lilly was so into praising God at this moment in time. She had her hands up and was feeling the love and connection to her Father God when she heard the preacher say after he received another word from the Lord that somebody has cancer of the stomach and is being healed. Lilly felt irritated for one moment when he spoke those words and then she felt this being leave her stomach. She was stunned but remembered the doctor telling her he did not know if cancer had gotten to her stomach or not. Lilly realized that God had just healed her of stomach cancer too. She had no proof but Lilly got blown out of her chair to go up and testify that God had just healed her. She received healing for kidney stones that had her bound for years and she just knew she was the healed. She went up on stage. When Lilly came near the preacher she sensed something was not right but knew the anointing had been moving. She tried to put her finger on what she was spiritually sensing and all she could come up with was that something was not right in his life with God. It was a sense of the evil one who had some kind of a grip on him and Lilly picked it up. She realized later on that he was a prosperity preacher and they are off the scriptures. She believed that was what she was feeling that was not right. During the service, there was a woman behind them who fell to the ground and a demon was manifesting itself. She was screaming and Lilly who was so in the Spirit turned back towards the woman and lifted up her arm and said out loud, "come out of her." Immediately she stopped and was delivered. Lilly was in awe of what had just happened at this well-known preachers meeting. God used her to tell the demon to leave and it obeyed immediately. Lilly was so in awe and excited. She was really not of this planet earth, especially during this time, where there were hundreds of people who were all worshiping Jesus. The thing is, Lilly was of this planet earth, but she was also connected to this spiritual world that was very much a part of this planet earth too. She was just so connected to this spiritual realm that it made her seem like she was not normal. Lilly was definitely not what you call normal. She was blessed. Lilly had enough proof to know she was not some crazy but was really in touch with this world of spiritual beings. How awesome is that? Lilly was so aware of this realm now that when she would go places she would keep her focus off of this realm because she did not want to deal with all these demons. They would manifest around her anyway so she would do her best to ignore them. It was not as if she could go around casting out demons everywhere she went.

Lilly was having all these amazing things happen and still no family to be heard from. The hurt was there and she thought of her poor son out in the world without her in his life after so many years of being together. It was a terrible separation for her.

She cried a lot and prayed for God to heal him from all the hurt she had caused him because of falling in love with the musician. Her husband would tell her all the time it was not her fault what happened. They reacted in a very poor way he said and they had no reason to hate you because you were in grief and everyone handles grief their own way. Lilly would hear what he told her but still could not get beyond the fact that it was because of her that her son was so hurt. She felt for all the children but he was the youngest and the only one not married with a family. He was alone out there and it killed her soul when she would think about it. Lilly did not fall apart and neither did her son or the rest of the family. God was with them all and was teaching them all. Lilly grew spiritually and her life with the Lord was wonderful. She did have this emptiness in her soul though because none of her family was with her. None of them really understood where she was coming from at the time but she knew she was in the will of God. Years went by. The church was brought back to the house because she and the musician knew that it was supposed to be there where the land was behind them. They knew God would eventually make the way for them to purchase this land for the building of this community where His people would gather during the tribulation.

Lilly was speaking to the angels who were part of her life and the angels who were watching over the church. The conversations she did have always involved inspirational messages given to her or a question she had in what was going on in the spiritual realm that she needed to know. She had the encounters with the tree branches falling off when she prayed. What happened during these times when Lilly prayed and the branches would crash to the ground was absolute proof that there was some kind of power being generated from the prayer. To think that Lilly was standing and lifted up her arms and rebuked the evil one when this extremely large branch crashed right behind her and was so loud she nearly jumped out of her skin! What does all this mean? There were some amazing things happening and Lilly herself would just watch as God did these things when she would pray. Lilly believes the power of God from The Holy Spirit would send a rebuke and the evil one would have a fit and in anger would actually rip the branch or use the wind to bring such a force that things would break. It was just so incredible because Lilly was just

171

a normal person who was baptized with The Holy Spirit. That was what made her special. It was The Holy Spirit. She was so in love with the Lord.

It looks like Lilly has a demon. How could Lilly, this emerald-eyed beauty, have a demon? I cannot believe it. Do you remember in the beginning when Lilly went to the fire department dinner and got hypnotized? The man touched her shoulder when he did his thing. Lilly was handed a demon spirit that day and it sat on her shoulder creating tension all the time. Its personality was one of annoyance and fear and frustration and let me add stress, too. They are the complete opposite of the angels of God. How in the world did Lilly find out she had this evil being? She was sitting in her chair while her husband, the musician, was reading the scripture that was found floating in the water, Ezekiel 36:25-26. Do you remember the newspaper article that her late husband was given by God to show what the ministry was supposed to do and how The Holy Spirit comes upon us? This scripture in Ezekiel says that the Spirit will sprinkle clean water upon us and cleanse us from all our filthiness and take away the stony heart from us and give us a heart of flesh. When the musician began to read this scripture verse Lilly began to feel very agitated. She was trying to figure out what was going on and realized it must be a demon. Something was motivating her with these feelings that she had not had a few minutes before. These annoyed feelings came out of nowhere and Lilly could feel exactly what this demon was feeling. It was as if Lilly herself had these emotions but she knew within her own soul that she had absolutely no reason to feel this way. They had been talking about the Lord and Lilly was feeling the love she had for God when out of nowhere her emotions turned from peace and joy to this creepy sensation of wanting her husband to shut up. She got really freaked out when she started to feel this entity motivate her to be angry. Lilly got scared and embarrassed all at the same time but did not want this thing near her so she told her husband she thinks she has a spirit. The musician very calmly said, "alright." and he got up and came over to her and began to pray. If you still believe Christians cannot have demons just read on and see what poor Lilly witnessed first-hand. From Lilly's own mouth came the words, "I do not want to leave." Lilly heard these very words come

172

out of her mouth and she became very upset and frightened. Lilly knew what to do as she had prayed for others to be delivered over the years so it was not as if she had no idea what to do. Lilly spoke to it and told it that it had to leave in the name of Jesus. It responded by saying, "I have been here for many years and it is your fault that I came." Lilly was trying to think of what she had done to allow this demon into her life. Lilly didn't have to think at all because the demon said, "you never repented from getting hypnotized and I am not leaving." Lilly got stern and said, "you are leaving." With those words the demon made Lilly scream in fear and Lilly was astonished at what was going on. It was scary because this thing was actually speaking through her and it did not want to leave. Every time it was rebuked by either the musician or Lilly herself, in the name of Jesus, it screamed and Lilly was so freaked out she was crying. She could feel it and she could feel her own emotions. It had a grip on her and she was telling it to go and it was fighting back. Lilly was making all kinds of faces as the demon was manifesting through her. She did not know what to do because it did not want to leave and she was commanding it to go in the name of Jesus and it was still tormenting her. Lilly was truly afraid and that was not what she should have been feeling, but the demon was scared and she felt scared and who knows which one was frightened the most. Lilly was so creeped out that this spirit was on her that she could barely say anything. She did not know why the demon did not go yet and this made her even more upset. What seemed like an eternity to Lilly was actually only a few minutes? After realizing this demon was fighting to stay, Lilly cried out to Jesus to please help her. As she was weeping in fear Lilly said, "Jesus I am so sorry for doing what I did. I had no idea it was wrong to be hypnotized and this spirit is holding onto me. I need your help, Jesus. Jesus help me!" Some of you might not believe this but just when Lilly called on the name of the Lord. Lilly actually saw Jesus walking towards her. The proof that this was really happening was when the demon screamed out, "Oh know it's the Lord, I'm leaving." He screamed loudly as he left and Lilly went limp. She was emotionally freaked out but what truly touched her heart was that Jesus, the Lord, her savior had actually taken the time to show up when Lilly could not help herself. Lilly was so overwhelmed with the love of Jesus and her life became even more intense in the world of the Kingdom of God. She was relieved to see that Jesus actually came to her. He is a present help in time of trouble just like His word tells us! Lilly saw it happen right in front of her very eyes. She saw him and the demon ran. She was utterly stunned by the whole ordeal and had a first-hand experience with these creepy beings. Once again she was rescued by God. She truly knew that she owed God everything for all that He had done for her. Lilly was so in love with the Lord. This deliverance made her even more in love with Him because she witnessed first-hand the kind of Lord He was. He is one that would never leave her nor forsake her. Unbelievable but true, never the less!

She lives every day in thanksgiving for the freedom God has given her. Now Lilly knows for sure Christians can have demons. She was a preacher and one who delivers people from demons and she herself was in need of deliverance from a spirit that latched onto her years ago when she allowed a hypnotist to touch her. How disturbing is that? It is truth my friends and we better take a deeper look into this spiritual realm so we can get free. Lilly realized now why she struggled so much with getting annoyed so easily and getting frustrated so easily. It was not her; it was the personality of the demon. I want to say here that Lilly was a very loving person to all and nobody really knew how she got tormented from time to time by this demon because they were just feelings that Lilly would do her best to ignore. The demon never held her back because Lilly learned very early in her walk with God that feelings meant nothing. Belief meant everything. She felt good now in her emotions. She could have peace now. Check out your emotions and see if you have issues that just seem to plague you. Could be one of these creepy impy looking things. Do not be afraid. They have to leave when told to in the name of Jesus. Lilly called upon the name of the Lord to help because it is kind of intense when you are involved in doing it yourself. The musician was helping too but Lilly is the one who mostly deals with demons so she basically was the one telling it to leave. It shows you how serious these beings are in their quest to stop the children of God. They need bodies to function and they do not care what body, as long as they find one, that is vulnerable or in sin which gives them access. Ignorance gives them access too. We

174

must remember that Lilly was a bit traumatized by this but she was learning. She really felt righteous anger at these creatures for their boldness in tormenting God's children. Lilly was going to help set the captives free. She grieved for the children of God who were mentally ill and living their lives with demons who just took over and buried the real person inside. So sad. Lilly knew many mentally ill people who loved the Lord. They all manifested when they were near her. One man every time she would run into him in town he would fall to the side and begin complaining about his back. It was routine and it was always the exact same thing. He acted out about how bad his back was and would sway back and forth saying how bad it was. It was so obliviously a demon because it was exactly the same each time she ran into him. It was so sad but Lilly could do nothing about it. He was so full of demons he was constantly talking to himself. He was a believer in Jesus but had been traumatized years ago from an accident and fell apart emotionally and ended up like this. There was no more of his personality it was all these demons acting out. Lilly would say hi to him and talk a few minutes as she walked by. It was really a conversation with demons. The Lord loves him and one day he will be free. Life moved on for Lilly and she was very busy doing the work of the Lord.

I have to make you see that just because Lilly operates in this spiritual realm with demons she also encounters the angels too. Deliverance which is what it's all about involves the demons. Lilly sees the demons so she can rebuke them and set people free. Her world of the spiritual involves the angels too. We would much rather hear about them but her life involves both. Here are a few more stories about the good side of this battle. By the way, have I told you we are in a battle? I'm pretty sure I have but just to remind you, we are in a real battle between good and evil. Be aware of it and stay on the side of good which is God. Time is running out on planet earth as we know it so now is not the time to walk into darkness. Stay in the light of the Lord and He will see you through the rough times ahead of us as we will enter into the tribulation.

Lilly encounters an angel while she is praying in the back yard. She and the musician were praying and an angel appears before Lilly and tells her he is bringing them tidings of great joy.

175

Lilly gets so moved in the spirit by this visitation and they both can feel the power of God as the angel stands before them. Lilly knows already that angels have been on the property behind their house. It is quite obvious in this realm of the spirit that God has chosen this land for Himself. Every time they go out back they can feel the presence of God. It comes off the hill and they know that God is going to have them buy this property to build this community for the Lord's people. Lilly is not good at waiting for anything so it is hard having to wait for all these things to be fulfilled.

Lilly sees another angel in their living room one day and she could tell it was a bit different than the others. It looked like it was ready for battle and Lilly asked who he was. He told her, "I am here to protect." She asked him what his name was and she got the name Cleondra. Lilly could see the difference between the warrior angels and the inspirational angels. The warriors were built more solid looking and were stronger in dominance. Hard to explain but they were like rougher in personality in a good way. Obviously, they were not going to take any garbage from any demon. The angels that Lilly encountered that were for inspiration were more delicate in nature and I do not mean to say that with disrespect but they were more feminine acting than the warrior angels. They have no gender but as far as the way they look the warriors act more masculine in personality than the inspirational ones do. That is really the only way Lilly could describe the difference and they all looked like men rather than women. Cleondra was ready to do battle while Petros was there to protect too but in the way of keeping Lilly and the musician in the Spirit by inspiration. Petros was very delicate in how he danced and Cleondra looked like he couldn't do a very good job of dancing but had a great ability to kick the demons across the planet if you know what I mean. Just like us the angels are all different and have different assignments to do in this world. We are all part of the same Kingdom and whether we know it or not they are working right alongside us to build up this army of people that God is teaching. I call it boot camp right here on earth. It is hard and can be very upsetting at times but in the end we will all be ready to be the true bride of the Lord. We can complain all we want but it will get us nowhere in our journey here on earth. We have to stop taking things personally because it is not personal. It is about good and evil and who is going to win. evil still thinks it has a chance. The bible already tells us the end of the story for the children of God. We will be persecuted on earth and we always have been since the beginning. Some of these preachers have taken the suffering that comes along with being a Christian and have told people that we are God's children and we should never be sick and never be poor and we should all be healthy, wealthy and enjoy. That is so opposite the word of God and over the years Lilly, who grew up with this prosperity message would wonder why she was struggling with money and dealing with afflictions here and there. After many years she finally found out the truth. They were preaching a false gospel of giving and you will get rich. It just tickles the ears and people give them all kinds of money because the selfishness of man wants to get rich. It plays on our greed of giving to get. Lilly never gave them money to get anything and it made her feel very guilty when all they would say was they never get sick and they were all very rich. Lilly was seeing all kinds of miracles and angels and yet she was poor and fighting off afflictions just like everybody else was. She used to wonder what she was doing wrong. She was actually doing everything right and the devil was trying to keep her back. Walking in the Spirit of the Living God makes us unattached to this life. There is no need for anything accept our daily bread. Any focus on getting rich and buying all these material things is not from the word of God. We are in this world but not of this world. It means what it says. The shaking that is coming is going to shake the Christians back into the Kingdom or they are going to walk away thinking God has forsaken them. Lilly heard the voice of God a few months ago say, "Lilly, from here on in do not take anything that is going to happen personally." In other words, do not get personally offended about anything that is going to happen. If we do not heed those words we will fall away from God. When the tribulation comes if we have believed we are getting out scot-free in the rapture and then nobody leaves, many children of God, will be so offended they will walk into the world. This seems harsh but it is going to separate the ones who are truly in love with Jesus from those who are in it to get what they can get from God. True love expects nothing and gives everything. When both sides give everything nobody lacks. We as the children of God are supposed to be giving our entire self to God. Not just the part we want to but all of us. The bride of Jesus will love Him through suffering just because they are so in love they cannot even imagine any other life but being with God, Jesus and the Holy Spirit for eternity. This life is too short to blow it and end up with the evil one because we could not lay our lives down for Him the way He laid His life down for us. Lilly wants to shine for the Lord not for herself. That is why she has been picked to be this emerald-eyed beauty who everyone looks at and wonders what it is about her that makes them feel so wonderful when she speaks words of wisdom and encouragement. The story goes on and remember, all of this world is infiltrated by other unseen spirits that are also living for a purpose. It is either a good purpose or a bad purpose. Lilly wants so much for you all to believe because she knows how important knowing about this part of Gods' Kingdom will be when the evil one has taken over as the anti-Christ. He will have his day and the Christians had better look deep within a person to know whose side they are on. In the last days, the word tells us we will be turned in by our family members because of their unbelief and thinking they are doing the right thing. We better have this gift of discerning spirits functioning so we can know what their soul is really all about. It is for divine protection. We will need to know who we can trust and who we cannot. Do not mean to make you fearful. Lilly does not want to deal with the tribulation either but we will all have to. Better to be prepared than to be caught off guard. Lilly is trying to make you see this world around us is very real and it is this spiritual world of evil that is going to motivate the anti-Christ and all manner of evil. Demons are behind the men who are taking the Christians and cutting their heads off. We better stop being afraid of them and take our stand as the army of the Lord. We have been given the power of the Holy Spirit with FIRE! What does fire do? It consumes everything in its path. Don't forget that it just might save your life one day. It did with Lilly more than once when death was waiting at her door. Never underestimate the power of our Father, GOD. Time to stand tall as the children of the MOST HIGH GOD!

   demons in daycare. Yes, you read it correctly. Children can have these imps too. Have to put this in the book because this

178

was so weird and disturbing but it really did happen just as I am going to tell it. I am telling you it will be hard for you to believe this, but Lilly really did experience this. The mother of the child could not believe it. Once again I assure you that it happened and the musician was there to witness this himself too. The other child in daycare also witnessed this and became fearful after she heard her fellow daycare friend say what she said and do what she did. The child was only four years old and Lilly knew she had some emotional issues from the beginning. The child would stare at her and Lilly knew she had a demon. That was not abnormal for Lilly so she just kept a watch on her like she did all the children. It was not as if the child was doing anything wrong. Lilly just knew that emotionally things were not quite right. One day Lilly noticed her dog chewing something so she went over and pulled it out of her mouth. She was still a puppy so everything went in the mouth. It was a twisty tie from a loaf of bread. Lilly said out loud, "that is not good, the dog can choke on this." Lilly wondered how the dog found it and she figured she must have dropped it. She thought to herself that she would have to be more careful because if the dog ever swallowed this thin wire it could get stuck in her throat. The next day she sees the dog chewing something again. She walks over and takes out another twisty thing from the bread out of her mouth. Lilly stopped and said to herself, "that is really weird, how is this dog getting these ties?" She did not want to have any incidents with the dog where she would have to bring her to the vet. Lilly did not have the money to do that, so once again she thought she better check the floor to see if there were any more of them. She did not find any more. The next day comes and once again the dog had one of these twisty ties in her mouth. Lilly was now ticked off about this and there had to be some explanation. All of a sudden she got a word of knowledge and knew what was happening. She knew without a doubt that this child was throwing them on the floor. Children play with things and can leave them around, so she would have to ask her about it. The ties were being stripped of the paper that covers them leaving only the wire part, so whoever was doing this was actually taking the time to pull off the paper covering so just the wire would be exposed. Lilly was going to find out if it was this child. The next day she says to the child, "I think I found one of your tie things on the floor from the loaf of bread." The child then point blank said to Lilly, "I put it there on purpose so your dog would eat it and die." Lilly was shocked. She said to the child, "why would you want to make the dog die?" She answered, "I do not like the dog and I just want her to die." Lilly thought. "wow, this is great, what do I do about this?" She proceeded to tell Lilly that she did the same thing to her dog. When Lilly asked her if she loved her dog she said, "she wanted it to die and if it did her mother would just buy her another dog." Lilly told her, "I do not think if you killed your dog your mother would buy you another dog. It is wrong to kill the dog or even try to." Lilly said. She then went on to say that if she got mad at the other child in daycare she would stab her with a knife. Lilly looked at the other child, whose eyes were now as wide as could be with fear. The child then went on and said something that made it quite obvious it was a demon manifesting itself. Remember this was a four-year-old child. The child began to smirk and say, "we are going to take over the world with magic." It was talking about its plans for taking over the world, which is the plan of the anti-Christ, the takeover of planet earth. It proceeded to show its hatred to people and animals and Lilly knew this child was no longer welcome to come back to daycare. The demons just cannot help themselves when in the presence of those who have The Holy Spirit. Lilly had to call her mother and the mother pretty much ignored Lilly and tried to act like this was normal. The child lied to the mother telling her she never said it, but there were three witnesses that day who heard it all. The other child had to be talked to about what happened because this just blew her away and from that moment on they were separated and never really hung out together. The family life of this child was obviously not good and the mom was upset when Lilly told her she could not come back to daycare. The mom got angry but Lilly told her that the child said she wanted to kill her dog and the child four times put this twisty thing on the floor to make the dog choke. Lilly told her this is a threat. She talked about the knife and how the child said she would stab the other child. Lilly told her she needed some serious counseling. Lilly knew it was demonic but you just cannot go around telling people their children have demons at the age of four. Lilly did pray for one other child in daycare who had a problem of jealousy with her sister and after

Lilly prayed the child was better. Children have emotions and the demons do not care who they attack. Lilly remembered one night many years before when her older son had a real episode of rebellion. It came out of nowhere and Lilly rebuked it immediately and it stopped. So children can have these imps attack them. The only way they really stay and actually connect with a person is if they walk into some sin and allow it to continue. If a person dabbles into the enemy's territory they are free pickings. Stay away from the devil and sin. It is not worth the torment and bondage he will put us through. The way of peace is through Jesus.

After years of not speaking to her son, they finally connected. Her daughter began to talk to her again too. Lilly trusted that God would bring healing because she knew she had been obedient to Him in this, and He would not allow her family to stay away forever. Healing was taking place and the devil was angry. Lilly invited her son to come for Christmas Eve, and when you hear what happened you will see that some things are just not a coincidence. Lilly and her husband, the musician, have been preparing for what they believe will be a struggle that this country is going to go through. They made a music CD and have been serving the Lord waiting patiently for God to make His moves to buy the land that borders their house which is the church too. Lilly's son came home that day and he was standing in the room talking to Lilly and all of a sudden the lights began to flicker. It was like the electric was being drained and they kept going on and off, on and off, very rapidly. Lilly looked at her son and said, "what is that?" With that, they hear this loud boom and the house shook. Lilly thought of her husband who was outside at the time and she ran to the door to see where he was in all this commotion. He was up on the hill with the chickens. Lilly walked out the door and the electric box was torn off the side of the house with the wires exposed and a huge tree had come down at the corner of the property. The tree had pulled the wires down. It was a tremendous gust of the wind that came with such fury that the tree was downed and the electric box that is made of metal was actually ripped off the side of the house. Lilly knew immediately what it was. She looked at her son and said, "this is because you are here and the devil is angry." The plan of satan was being foiled by the reconnection of Lilly and her son. They went five days without

181

lights and thanked God that the winter was so mild they did not have any problem not having heat. They thanked God nobody was hurt and it was a good experience for Lilly and the musician to see what it would be like living by candles. There were no Christmas lights for them but there was a breakthrough in the spiritual realm. The devil was ticked off and Lilly knew it. They also had no money to have the electric box fixed and for a few moments Lilly wanted to go into panic mode but said to herself, "God is bigger than this problem and He will make the way for us." Lilly picked an electrician from the phone book that she felt The Holy Spirit was telling her to call. The man showed up after Christmas and gave the estimate which was six hundred dollars. Lilly, feeling very embarrassed, told the man she had no money to pay him at that time and God moved the man to do it and allow them to pay it off. It was repaired with absolutely no money down and believe me that was an answer to their dilemma of no money and no electricity. Before this event happened one of the church members was having a recurring dream. Because of her ignorance to the gifts of The Holy Spirit, she did not tell the pastors. It was given to her two times and she ignored it. It was the devil who needed to be rebuked because he was planning an attack on the pastors. If they had been told this word from the Lord this attack might not have happened. We must be vigilant in our walks with God. The gifts of the Spirit are for our benefit while we are here in this messed up world. We need all these gifts operating in the children of God or we will miss messages that need to be said and rebukes that need to be spoken.

Lilly gets told by God that her son is going to move back into the house. Lilly knew it would be challenging with his dog and her dogs that they breed to help the ministry feed the needy. She also knew God had a reason for it. Things were getting closer to the time of building this place of refuge. Her son must have something to do with this blessing coming to pass. She had connected with a friend from way back who was in her wedding party with her late husband. She was also believing about these places of refuge and started to get moved by God to be part of this. She was going to sell her house and come and move with all of them to live in this place of safety. Things were beginning to fall into place. Sure enough, Lilly had heard correctly because her son moves back into the house. The first thing Lilly saw when helping him move back was the message from the water that her late husband had been given to by God. Lilly realized it left with her son and now it was coming back to the location where this place was meant to be built. It was not a coincidence and Lilly was excited. Her son was not so thrilled about it because he wanted to be on his own. Lilly told him that the next time he leaves it will be for the right reasons not because the devil attacked everybody.

Lilly has been finding dimes on the ground everywhere she goes. She knows God is telling her that He is going to make the way to build this place. As exciting as it is the doubts are always there to try to take away your belief in something. The mind is enmity against God so we cannot listen to the mind. We have to listen to the heart which is where The Holy Spirit is. Lilly prays all the time about this vision and expects it to happen. She knows how to wait for God to bring to pass a vision. She waited about seven years to get pregnant with her son and the devil tormented her with it. She would not sit and dwell on this vision of the place of refuge. God would do it when He was ready. No sense in getting tormented about it. She refused to listen to the thoughts that would tell her it is never going to happen. She also had visions of this place and although Lilly hates to wait, she knew God was in control of the timing and that it was real.

Things in the world have been escalating. This is the year 2016 of the Jewish Jubilee and it is predicted that the economy might fall apart. Lilly has no money to really prepare the way she wants to and it is very frustrating for her. She bought what she could. Most Christians think those who are looking to store up food etc., are off the scriptures. The whole Noah story lines up with what Lilly and others are looking to do. The musician comes to Lilly and tells her that the paper from the water that God gave her late husband talks about Noah. Lilly had never realized that because her late husband only focused on the scripture he was reading at that time, he had folded the paper up so that only one part of the message could be seen. When Lilly opened it up and saw the part about Noah and the Ark she got very excited. This really makes it obvious what God is doing. Then Lilly gets hit with the realization that this message was floating in the water like Noah's Ark was. They ended up in this house because of what? A flood! Lilly started to get so excited she absolutely knows that no way all these situations that have happened are a coincidence. God is on the move. All the dimes being found represent the number ten which could mean Noah too because he was the tenth generation and Noah means rest. There are two meanings of Noah that are going on here. One as in, the days of Noah so too shall the coming of the son of man be. Jesus is coming and things will be like in the days of Noah when man is doing his own thing without God. There will be these places that Lilly and the musician are calling Tribulation Arks, safe havens, places where God's people will dwell until He returns. While the tribulation is going on these places will be protected by angels. God's purposes will be fulfilled in this world. He will have the last say in spite of how society is slapping Him in His face.

It is amazing that during the finishing up of this book Lilly continues to see visions. Once again I have to include another vision into the story. This vision will make us all realize how close we may be to the second coming of Jesus. The year is still 2016 and this is the year of the elections in America. The country has been under a President who does not follow the words of the bible and the Supreme Court voted to change the status of marriage to allow same sex marriage to be legal. Lilly is watching the decline of the country and has been very upset about it. Much prayer has been going up for the country to turn around and come back to God and His laws for the land, not what man decides. With all this on her heart Lilly wakes up one morning and finds herself in a vision. She was above the clouds in an angelic realm. She could feel the presence of the angels all around her as she seemed to be floating in the air with them all. She had peace and just waited for a moment until she heard the words coming directly from God. He said in a voice that was spoken from one who had authority, " Trump is sounding the trump for the second coming of Jesus. She then heard God tell her, "Trump has been being prepared for this his whole life and is called to be the President for this very moment in time." At that point, as Lilly was still lying on her bed, she knew Trump was picked by God to be President. She was not told he was going to win but she knew he was chosen by God. She could only surmise from what was said that he would be the one to win in the election and the reason for

God's choice was to help restore the damage that was done. His talents are all about restoration as he is one who fixes buildings and restores things and is an expert in making trade deals.

Lilly has a prophetic dream. It is a word from the Lord and one that she does not want to see happen. In the dream, she is walking down a road with buildings. She looks down the road and sees a street sign. It says N.Y. and under that she sees 8.9 earthquake and under that again she sees N.Y. As she is looking at it, she looks up at the sky and sees clouds like a storm is coming. Behind the clouds, she knows God is there and she sees Him pointing to the sign. He is telling her that He is showing her this because it is going to happen. Lilly wakes up immediately. She is thinking of this dream and how it does not seem possible but she knows the dream was God actually showing her it is going to happen. When Lilly has dreams from the Lord she wakes right up from them and knows they are from God. The next day Lilly goes on the internet to see if anybody else has had a vision of this earthquake coming to New York City. The N.Y.N.Y. meant New York City. Lilly does find two other pastors who have been told the same thing. They were told it was going to be a large magnitude just like Lilly was told. Lilly put it out on Facebook but nobody will believe her. That was always part of the frustration of being a prophet of the Lord. People just think you're crazy until it all happens. Lilly has seen enough miracles to know that it is all true. The world is in for a great shaking and hopefully many will come to the Lord. In the last days, many will walk away because they will not stand fast with their God and Jesus. They will go by their emotions and fall to the wayside. Lilly gets so grieved about it. This book is not to glorify Lilly even though people look in awe when such miracles happen through people. It is to get the truth out; that there are children of God who walk with the power of The Holy Spirit and can see the spiritual world. Lilly wants people to know it is truth and that these amazing stories are real.

Lilly gets a feeling when she drops off a woman from church to go and pray for her son. She did not want to bother him because she did not know if he was a believer but she knew he was not in very good shape physically. Lilly does not go and pray for him but she prayed silently to God about the situation he was in. At this time Lilly and the family did not know how bad he actually was. That very day he is rushed to the hospital and his girlfriend is told that he might not make it. She calls Lilly and cries and Lilly asks her if she can pray for him. She welcomed the prayers and Lilly asked God if He would save his life. Sometimes Lilly knows and sometimes she does not know what God is going to do. She did her best to comfort the woman and that was all. Within a few days, he showed remarkable improvement and his doctor told her it was a miracle of God because he was dying. Once again Lilly was used for stopping death. Lilly was happy for her. This was not the end of her problems because this woman who asked for prayer found a lump on her breast. The biopsy showed it was the big C, cancer. The word nobody wants to hear. She calls Lilly and tells her and Lilly immediately gets a knowing that this cancer was going to leave. She was prayed over and the cancer was rebuked in the name of Jesus. Lilly had gotten what is called a word of knowledge from the Holy Spirit that the cancer would be gone. When she went in to have it removed it was no longer cancer. There is a well-known physician in this town where Lilly lives who bears witness to these healings as he has watched these miracles happen right in front of his eyes. God is a healer and is still healing today in this world we all live in.

Lilly's stories and experiences will go on until she goes home but this book was written while Lilly was bedridden with a back issue and could not walk without pain. The Lord told her He was using this back issue so she would finish writting this book. Lilly sat day after day in pain as this story was written about her life. When the book was nearly done Lilly miraculously recovered from her inability to walk around without pain. Think about this for one minute. She is basically bed ridden because of the severe pain she gets when walking. God tells her to finish writing a book that had been started back in 2001 and then sat on the shelf for fifteen years. The only relief from pain was to sit in bed and not move the leg and back. Walking put pressure on the sciatic nerve and the knee and ankle just could not be walked on. Lilly hobbled around the house in severe pain doing the daily chores that had to get done, but the rest she left. Six to seven hours a day the book was being written, because timing is very critical and everything that needs to get done must be finished on the schedule of God.

Lilly received a word from the Lord about her back and leg. He told her that once the book was done she would be healed. God lovingly told her that because she was such a go-getter and never sat still, He had to use this affliction to keep her dormant until the book was finished. Lilly knew what He meant and she accepted the task of completing her story. During that fifteen years, the book was meant to sit in waiting until Lilly matured into this emerald-eyed beauty who was meant to talk with the angels. Her life is an example to all so the children of God will know that Jesus Himself walked with this gift and could see and talk to angels. Enoch also talked with the angels. Can anyone really say that all these things are nothing but coincidence? For three weeks Lilly sat in bed and finished the story about her life. God told her to write it and she did. What God does with it is His business. Lilly will acknowledge the awesomeness of her God and when He says something is going to happen it does. The pain just left as soon as she finished writing the book and all that Lilly did was obey what He told her to do.

One more amazing thing happened while this book was being completed. Lilly's husband has to go to the emergency room because of a bad reaction to some medication he had to take. Lilly got very upset about it because his heart was doing all kinds of weird stuff that it should not have been doing. It brought Lilly back to the death of her husband years before and she went into a bit of panic mode. She was in a battle with fear. The impy demon flew right next to her and would not shut up all night as it tormented her soul. Lilly kept rebuking it and had to keep saying out loud that God was in control and all things work together for good. It was a real battle of the mind. It was the demon against Lilly's faith. Lilly felt physically ill from the tormenting fear. She went on Facebook to ask everyone to pray. She noticed her friend was up so she quickly told her what happened. She got a response back very quickly which said," Lilly I know you are upset, but your husband is going to be alright." The message did not say, husband, it actually said his name which has been kept out of the book. Lilly got really touched by this because she truly felt it was a word from the Lord spoken by her friend. Lilly proceeded to write some more things back in response to what her friend had said. Lilly thought it very odd when her friend did not write anything else back to her.

187

Lilly thought to herself, "how could she go offline just when I am talking to her. She answered me back with those words of encouragement and knew I was upset so why would she go off at that moment in time?" Lilly was confused but it was late so she figured maybe she just answered her quickly and went to bed. Lilly did not think that was something she would do, especially when Lilly was so upset. It did not make any sense and Lilly even thought maybe she was busy doing something else and would come back and talk to her. Her friend never said another word. What she did say was enough to help Lilly calm down a bit. Lilly was truly attacked that night but got through it. The next day Lilly goes online and sees that many wrote back to let her know they were praying. Her friend writes to her and tells her that she was sorry that she did not see what Lilly wrote that night because she was sleeping. Lilly answered back and said, "what do you mean you did write to me?" Her friend said, "no, I was sleeping and my computer just does not show when I am off-line." Lilly then tells her, "You wrote me back last night and it touched my heart." Her friend said it was not her and Lilly wondered how did she get this message then? As Lilly thought about it she then realized the only explanation was that it had to have been God or an angel who had answered her back. Lilly checked all the messages from people and thought maybe it was from someone else but nobody else sent it either. Lilly went back to re-read what she wrote to her friend and then noticed that she had sent a reply back which had to mean she had read something that was sent to her. There were no messages showing so Lilly actually responded to no one. When Lilly realized it had to be God who sent it she was so lifted up that fear left. While her husband was in the hospital having his heart completely checked out both Lilly and her husband were getting moved by The Holy Spirit. The hours driving every day that Lilly did was filled with praise music and prayer and Lilly was expecting God to heal her husband one way or the other. The God of the universe had loved her enough to speak to her and comfort her soul by a supernatural message on Facebook. Lilly was so moved in her soul that there were no words to even say. Once again her God had stepped into her humanity and encouraged her. This happened just before this story was to be finished, and Lilly was in bed right before that for a few weeks, forcing her to stay still long enough for this story to be written down, so all the world can see how God really does care about His children, and does give supernatural abilities to help His people. Lilly's life is so busy that having to stay in bed was just what the doctor ordered for her recovery and for your enjoyment. The day that the musician was to have the dye put into his heart Lilly was in deep prayer and as they wheeled him into the room. Lilly walked away with tears in her eyes as she told him she loved him. Lilly was alone in the waiting room because it was very late and her husband had to wait from twelve midnight until five PM. without eating or drinking anything. It was a long day of waiting and keeping a focus on God rather than the not knowing what they would find. Lilly had already prayed against stents having to be put in as she felt led by The Spirit to do. When you are under tremendous stress the emotions run very high and that is when we are most prone to attack from the enemy. There were so many prayers going up that the devil could not get a foothold. He tormented Lilly the first night, but after that his power was thwarted by the power of God. Lilly did everything she felt the Holy Spirit told her to do. The time to find out what was going on was now while she was waiting in the room. Lilly looked up to heaven and spoke to God one last time before they would find out. In all sincerity Lilly said these words to her God, "I will appreciate whatever way you heal my husband, but I have to admit Lord I will be disappointed if he has to have stents put in. He is too young and so talented and has much work to do for you it just does not feel like that is what should happen." "Father we love to see miracles happen down here because they are very exciting for us and they show your awesome power." I have asked in the name of Jesus and you say if any two of us agree as to touching anything that you will do it and I have agreed with other people for him not to need these stents." I will be thankful no matter what because you are God and you do know what is best for our lives." Lilly told the Lord she loved Him and waited as patiently as she could. The doctor came out very quickly and Lilly felt that it was too short of a time if they had to put anything in so she felt an excitement as the doctor approached her. He told her, "his heart is clean as a whistle." Lilly lifted up her hands in thanksgiving to God. The doctor told her, "I do not understand because the stress test showed some issues." Lilly said. "it is God" and she thanked and hugged the doctor. She did not know what the doctor believed but she gave a witness to all around her of how God had healed her husband. This is another amazing part of the life of Lilly. Lilly was not able to walk while this book was being written and just before finishing it she got healed and then her husband had this happen. The final parts of the story are being written. The enemy will try to stall things and stop things from happening but God always wins. This attack against her husband was a demonic one because the job where her husband was working was creating stress, as the environment was not one of peace but anxiousness from the boss to all working for him. The finances got so bad that the musician went to make some money so they could pay the bills. While he was working very hard and feeling all the worldly pressure and disrespect from the boss he was attacked in his emotions by this spirit of stress and the need to finish all this work every day. Pressure, pressure, pressure creates anxiety and allows the enemy to come in and push us to feel overwhelmed and anxious. Too much stress can cause the heart to react and that is why we need to notice when we are not acting like our normal selves. Lilly could feel the difference in his behavior but did not know herself that it was a demon. The plan was to stop the book and the moving forward of building this place of refuge for the children of God. The devil was ticked off once again. The musician noticed the demon when it showed itself while he was watching a Christian show in the hospital. The spirit left and the musician was healed. God is good and we must recognize these spiritual beings that do exist and are meant to destroy our lives.

Lilly's entire life has been to bless others and in doing that she receives blessings too from her God. The message from the sea over thirty years ago is about to happen. America has turned away from the one true God and things are about to get bad. Many do not want to believe it but the true prophets will be recognized at some point in time. The nothing-but-the-fun-gospel is from the pits of hell. It is self-focused and it is not biblical. It is not all about having fun and getting all these material things so we can be happy. It should be about laying down our lives for Jesus and following Him into His kingdom right here on earth. America is about to get woken up. It might even happen before this gets published. The power of God is real and The Holy Spirit is wanting to take over the children of God and lead them to all truth.

Lilly just found out that the land they are waiting to buy is still up for sale. They were coming back from town and there was a sign with the 49 acres. This is the fifty-year Jubilee and Lilly thinks this will be the year the land will come back to God for His people. She is waiting! Lilly woke up and realized that the 49 acres for sale would be connected to their one acre making the total 50 acres. The year of jubilee. Coincidence? I think not. One more confirmation. I will end with this amazing part of the ending.

God is involved in our names and birthdays more than we know. Lilly's husband, who passed away, had a last name that meant and with these hands. Lilly's name means bird in German. The musician's initials mean refuge. A vision was given by God of how He wanted the ministry sign to look. The sign has large hands reaching out from the sky and there is a dove in the middle being released. The ministry sign represents two things. It shows the hands of God releasing His Holy Spirit in the form of a dove to the world. The ministry sign also represents Noah and the dove he releases to see when the waters were receded and of course they stayed in the Ark until the floods were gone as a place of refuge and rest. Noah's name means rest, which is what they did while they waited for the floods to recede. Lilly's husband dies and with his hands releases Lilly the dove who meets the musician, whose initials mean refuge, who is the one who will actually build the Ark. All the names fit into what actually happened in their personal lives for the place of refuge God had shown her late husband from the water all those years ago. Lilly had to be released from her husband in death to fly and meet the musician whose initials mean refuge because he is called of God to build this place. That is no coincidence and each person plays their part in what God has ordained to be. God says our steps are divinely ordered and this proves it. Three names that fulfill a vision. The son whose 24th birthday falls in Tishri 1 and 2 this year 2016 represents the beginning of a new time period beginning Oct 3-4th in 2016 which is his 24th birthday. This child of God who was prophesied to be born had a real purpose in the timing of all this. His being born dead and his coming back to life we believe represents the

United States and the collapse which would be death but it will come back to life just like Lilly's child did. The 124 that Lilly saw in the hospital while she was giving birth to her son means their birthdays, Jan. 4th, Feb. 4th, and Oct. 4th but it means more than that. Lilly did not know any of this until this book was being completed. It also means Tishri 1 and 2 on his 24th birthday is going to be a significant change in America. All these things in 2016 are the beginning of what lies ahead for the world. What will happen will make the Christians see that the true prophets of God are warning about what the book of Revelation tells us will take place so the people can get ready. This child was born to show what God was going to do and that is why the devil killed him. Death to life will happen to America. The numbers 124 also add up to the musician's birthday on the 7th which means completeness. His coming into the picture means the completing of the vision of this place of refuge which is exactly what his name means. Lilly's son's name is a combination of them all together. His name means, and with these hands, a gift from the Lord is given and I send my dove to lead you to the place of refuge where you will be safe until my return. It will be a new beginning for the children of God who find their way to this place or any of the other places that are all over the world. Lilly's son was given three names at birth plus his last name. Why? God must have influenced his parents to do it because he was sent to represent a time period of change that God was about to do in the world and America. You may say that is ridiculous because he is just an ordinary person. Read the bible because that is exactly who God chooses to use. The humble in heart. The ones who would rather sit in the back and remain silent. The ones who will not want to take the attention away from the one who truly deserves it, Jesus. This is why the return of Lilly's son was very significant in this. He had the paper from the sea and the split of the family was a spiritual attack to keep things hindered. Now you might be able to see why the devil went to such lengths to rip apart this family and try to kill all four of them before ever completing this grave undertaking of building what they are calling the Tribulation Ark. Are the children of God just ordinary people? No, they are not, for they house The Holy Spirit and He is anything but ordinary. He is the third person of the Trinity which means three in one.

His power is most amazing and He will come and use anyone who is humble enough and faithful enough to listen to Him. Lilly, her late husband, her son and the musician are all anointed by the MOST HIGH GOD to complete this message that was given from the water. It was floating in the water just like Noah's Ark was to show what was meant to happen at the exact moment in time when God would call His people to these safe havens. Lilly found this house, representing the dove, in search of dry land after their home was destroyed by a real flood in the year 2006 in the town God had sent them to. The number 46 ½ is the address of this home that Lilly found and believe it or not it means to be secure from the water or flood which represents chaos. Chaos will take place during the end time tribulation. The one acre they live on, connected to the 49 acres around their home, makes the total number of acres 50, representing the year of Jubilee which is 2016 and happening as this book is being written. The scripture which says in Isaiah about going behind closed doors while the wrath of God is poured out on the earth shows that these places are of the Lord and are being built everywhere. They will be ready in time for the last 3 ½ years of the tribulation which is when they will really be needed. The house they found, after the flood, with the 49 acres for sale, that is connected to their property with one acre, will be protected by God and His angels. The floods of life, the chaos, that is coming during the seven-year tribulation will be kept away from these areas that were shown to the prophets thirty years ago. Only the true bride of Christ will be led to these Arks. It will be just like the days of Noah and most people will laugh and think that Lilly and her fellow Ark community builders are nuts. It took Noah 120 years to build his Ark for the Lord but these Arks will go up very quickly when the time is right. Let me say here that these places of refuge will not look like a boat they are just being called Arks because they are safe places to live while the storm is raging with the wrath of God on the earth. Noah did not leave the planet when God poured out His anger. He went into a boat that was able to withstand the storm. That is why these places are being built in certain locations so if there is any flooding or earthquakes or volcanic eruptions they will be safe because the angels of God have been commanded to keep them protected. Lilly has seen the property and it is filled with angels already before they have even bought it. That must mean something in the spiritual realm. Lilly realized the other day that this generation is called Millennials. Her son who was prophesied to be born was born many years later after her first two children were born and this son is a Millennial. Jesus is coming back during one of the generations and is going to reign for 1,000 years which is called a Millennium. It is not a coincidence that this generation of Millennials will reign with Jesus for 1,000 years, a Millennium. Lilly got a revelation that they are the generation when Jesus will return. The Lord has dates and times set for things to happen and the Father knows the exact date. The children of God will know about the time He will return as the book of Revelation happens. Her son has emerald eyes too and Lilly just realized that he is called of God to be the generation of Millennials who will realize that Jesus is Messiah and is coming again. Lilly's generation is older and many will die before the return of the Lord but not the Millennials. It is very exciting to realize that her son is chosen and has the same color eyes as she has. What does it all mean? It means that God picks and chooses His prophets and they will fulfill their purpose on this earth. It is very exciting how God uses times and seasons and names and people all for His Glory! Jesus is coming back sooner than we think. Not before the tribulation either. It would be great if we all got out of here but just does not say that in scripture. What will happen? The safe places will be built for those who believe.

All the gifts that God gives His people will be what is used during this time when His wrath pours on the earth and His people once again are put into places of safety and refuge. This is the scripture that says it all. Isaiah 26:20-21 which says, "go, my people, enter your rooms and shut the doors behind you; hide yourselves for a little while until His wrath has passed by." See the Lord is coming out of His dwelling to punish the people of the earth for their sins. This is talking about the children of God going into places of refuge to hide while He, God, is punishing the sinners. They are calling these places His Arks of safety or tribulation Arks. Christian communities where everyone lives off the land and loves the Lord. Look up and see the signs of the times. We can discern the weather Jesus says in scripture but we cannot discern the signs of the end times. We are in the end times and if you read the book of Acts you will see how the church was meant to be and we will be going back to just how it was when Jesus first came and showed His people that He was the way, the truth, and the life!

My name is Marcos and I am an angel of the Most High God. I bear witness to the words written in this book and have been by Lilly's side since conception. I have watched her mature into the woman she is today and have seen her struggles and her sorrows. Lilly has been given humility and because she does not take the praises for God unto herself. She was chosen to be a vessel of honor for the Lord. I have stood by her side all these years and the years are but a moment in time which passes by very quickly. I remember the day she was born on that cold day in January and I did feel honored to be her guardian angel. I have watched the evil one do his best to not only destroy her life but to kill her. I have been in the presence of God always and as I look into this emerald-eyed beauties face and all I can see is Jesus. I never once looked at her and thought why did she do this or why did she do that. I already knew that evil has many ways of persuasion that are very seductive to humans and are almost impossible at times to resist. What I do know from being an angel and watching Lilly for so many years is that the human spirit of man is very strong and when they set their mind to something it can be accomplished through sheer will. Another thing I know about man, with that will if they would know the truth about God they would be unstoppable in this battle. We are all in this fighting for good and stopping evil. Lilly speaks to me and I speak to her. You might think that very strange or even impossible. I say to you if you are but a spirit in a body, then why not be able to connect to that side of your being and know what is happening to it. Why should any of you as spirit beings not be able to accept that part of yourselves and see us for who we are the same way we can see you for who you are. We are spirit and so are you. See me for who I am. Lilly does now after many years of being in the dark. She is moved by The Holy Spirit within her own human spirit and has been given the ability to know what we are doing. I have to say it is quite pleasing to me as an angel to be able to tell her something that she needs to know and have her hear what I have said. I am her guardian angel and my purpose is to watch over Lilly every day, every hour, and every minute of each day of her life. For eternity I will always feel a special bond between the two of us because most guardian angels never have the opportunity to speak to the person they are watching over. Lilly is chosen and is not the normal in this world but as children of God, every one of you can, through The Holy Spirit, experience some of these things that have happened to Lilly. Lilly is just the vessel being used by God to accomplish His mission of bringing salvation and love to His people who are lost and need to be found. I will conclude with this. My permission to do this comes from God because He truly wants His people to realize this spiritual realm not only exists but is vital in our battle against the evil one. You need the supernatural power of God to be part of your lives, and the angels will be helping guide you all in the right directions as the world gets darker and darker. The light of God will grow dim during this tribulation in the world but it will be shining very bright in these places of refuge where the angels of God will be dwelling to protect all those who God holds dear to His heart. Jesus came to set the captives free and we, the angels, will help bring that to pass. I, Marcos, have spoken the truth and the story of Lilly has now been shared and is no longer a secret. May the Lord of peace keep you safe and bring all the lost sheep back home again! I, Marcos, bare witness that this story is based on truth! Go and be with the Lord and may the God of peace shower you with the hope of Glory in Jesus Christ who is the King of Glory and is coming again! He is the way, the truth and the life and no man comes to the Father but by Him!

I am Lilly but Lilly is not my real name. This book, my story, has been written for one reason and one reason only, to show the children of God that His Spirit is still with us and doing wonderful things to deliver His children from harm and from evil, every day of our lives. God chooses how we look, how smart we may be, how tall or short we are and the color of our skin and our hair. The human race passes on personalities and facial features from one family to another. Each family has a certain look to them and character traits that develop. As the children of God, we were made in His image and likeness so technically we should look like God and act like God. If you truly believe that then every person should look to their Father up in heaven and know that God purposely created them to be like Him. Our outward appearance has nothing to do with the fact that we are made in His image. There are many different flowers in this world and colors and each is unique but they are all flowers. It is the same with mankind. Our spirit identifies who we really are and what facial features we have been given by God. He will use them for His purpose and His purpose alone if we let Him. The angels were not created in His image and likeness, only man was. The reason the true children of God were predestined to be conformed to the image of Jesus is because He is our brother and we are very much alike if we grab hold of The Spirit of God who comes into our human spirit to dwell and lead us to all truth. If we look at ourselves for who we really are our lives will not be anything like the world and all the people who reject God. Not all human beings are the children of God. Many have turned against their Father and have accepted the devil as their father. I learned many years ago that my Father God truly loves me and will never leave me nor forsake me. I also know that being human and having to live in a world where everything focuses on what our flesh wants can be very tempting. The truth is the only answer to real happiness and that truth is how much we are loved by God and that we are really in this world but very much not a part of it. When you understand that you will be able to walk in The Spirit of your Father God and live your life just for Him. That is when we find true joy.

Just because someone may think I am pretty, should I then exalt myself above others? I will not look in the mirror and say how wonderful I am. Did I have any say in how my flesh looks? Did the God of this universe not choose the way my eyes shine His glory? My eyes are green and the story is named because of their color, but did I take the colors of the rainbow and pick or choose how my eyes were created to gaze upon man? The noticing of my eyes has always been quite uncomfortable for me because I could sense the jealousy of others at times. It would upset my soul because it was not as if I had anything to do with it. I never thought of myself as beautiful but have been called beautiful by many over the years. Beauty is in the eye of the beholder and true beauty comes from within. There are many beautiful women in this life but the question is how do they treat their fellow human beings? I have run away from attention my whole life until my

197

Father God told me why He made me look the way I do. He told me that I had a purpose of showing people how much He loves them, and my face was being used by Him to draw people to look, so I could have an avenue to speak His truth. You see, even beauty has its purpose down here and it is not for our own self-ego or vanity. If a face has a certain appeal because it is unusual or just plain nice to look at and is admired by others, that is to the glory of God, not man. If a person has no outward beauty but has such inner warmth that will also draw people to themselves and they may glorify the God of this universe. I have always known that whatever gifts have been bestowed upon me by my God, in return, I am to use them for Him. I have been hiding most of my life with the belief that humility was to be silent and not do anything with these talents. The word tells us not to bury our talents but to do something meaningful with them. The enemy convinced me that I was not supposed to shine but hide and not be looked at. After all, if I was looked at because someone might think I am pretty that would be wrong. Why is it wrong? It only is wrong when pride comes in and makes us think we are above someone else because we are better than they are. I am humble in heart and true humility is not to hide your gifts and talents but to glorify God in them. Pride is puffing oneself up and making a wrong assessment of yourself. Humility is being able to see the talents you have been given and not bragging on them but recognizing that God gave them to you and be thankful for each and every gift. If people look at you because they like what they see you have the perfect opportunity to know that God is the creator of each one of us and molds us all into His image and likeness. The package we are in is not the important part but what the soul matures into, as one of His children. If I have been chosen to tell people how much God loves them and my face makes them notice me, then I have been given a tool, to do my job on this earth. I will not take any glory from my Lord who suffered and died for me. I had a real tough time deciding whether to even tell my story but God spoke to me and told me point blank to shine, shine, shine. I told my Lord I was sorry for feeling that I had to hide myself to be humble and I said if God wanted me to be known for His glory I would not stand in his way. I have put myself out for all the world to see that Jesus is the Christ and we do have The Holy Spirit with His

198

power and fire and I will shout it from whatever house top I can climb. If you look at me, you will see Jesus and that is my reason for writing my story! May the Lord Jesus touch all those who read this. I pray you will all believe me and recognize the truth as this world is so full of lies it is hard to know the difference these days. After my husband the musician had nothing wrong with his heart, when we all had been praying so hard for a miracle, I put the praise report out on Facebook. I also told how my son came back to life in this same hospital almost twenty-four years earlier. I got a response back from a woman who wrote, give me a break! It upset me because she was a Christian and it just showed me how many Christians do not even believe it possible for these amazing miracles to happen. Not only do they happen, they happen with just ordinary people who are in love with Jesus and take His word as truth. It breaks my heart that I have truly seen these most unbelievable miracles take place and yet there are those who think I am making it all up. To God be the glory because I owe Him my very life and will keep shouting His love to the world. This book is truth. I bear witness to it, the God of this universe bears witness to it, the Lord Jesus Christ bears witness to it, the Holy Spirit bears witness to it and the angels of the Most High God bear witness to it. Amen! This is not the end but the continuing of my life until I either go home or Jesus comes back. Those who are alive and remain at His coming will be changed in the twinkling of an eye and will be caught up together, with everyone else who believes and will meet Jesus in the clouds. This would be the rapture! I and all my brothers and sisters in the Lord will return with Him to dwell on the earth for a thousand years. Eternity has begun! This is the last chapter and it happens to be chapter eight which means new beginnings! God bless you all! Stay safe and may the power of The Holy Spirit touch your lives as it did mine! I will end with this word. God is truth and what I have told you in this book has been truth and I pray you believe it. May His glory shine upon His people in such a way that the world will look in awe, at the existence of God and Jesus whom He has sent!

Epilogue

I cannot end this story without saying this. Remember one thing in life, we are all sinners saved by the grace of God through the sacrifice of Jesus! There is no person on this planet earth who has arrived in their spiritual level where they cannot be sorely tempted of the devil and fall right on their face. If you think you are spiritual do not take that with pride but with the knowledge that the God of this universe is molding you into the image of His Son. The evil one has power and that power is very seductive in its ability to entice even the elect into its lies. If we do not keep a humble attitude we become like satan and pride comes before a fall. Never, ever underestimate your opponent and do not think you are so spiritual you cannot fall right on your face. We must diligently seek the Lord daily and thank Him for everything He provides for us. We must pray for one another and not judge each other for our shortcomings because the saying goes, there, but for the grace of God, go I.